LIFE IN THE FAST LANE

A JOURNEY BACK TO MYSELF!

By ZINALETRECE

Acknowledgements

I would like to thank my children, my parents, my cousin Kimberly and my aunt Renee. I'd like to also thank the communications department at Cal State Dominguez Hills, Jose Ballester Panelli (the artist that donated the interior art), Luis Ruben Rosado (without whom this book may never have been finished), and Treva, Lisa Leon and Cupcake Brown (who paved a path for me to follow) and last but certainly not least God who guided my pen every step of the way.

This book is dedicated to my children; Cedrick, DaWayne, Shawna, KeyAnna and Sabrina...It is my hope that my story encourages you as you journey on your own path!

TABLE OF CONTENTS

INTRODUCTION

I wrote this book 13 years ago and now, 13 years later, I have decided to publish it. Back then my genuine interest was to put into black and white what allowed me to have 13 years of an upright mind, soul and spirit. It was this spirit that moved my pencil.

Today, with 26 years of sober experience, I want to share with you "Life In The Fast Lane: A Journey Back To Myself". During this journey you may feel like a little boat traveling in a downhill, turbulent river. Sometimes you will feel weak, unprotected and lost but at the end you will find the golden place of self-discovery.

I have designed this journey in 11 chapters covering the span of my life from the mid 1960's, through the 1970's and ending in the 1980's. Each one is packed with events, people and places that effected a change in my life for the good over the last 26 years. Hopefully, as you journey with me through these chapters, my story will touch your heart effectively too.

For me to say anything, I'd have to say that the first 3 decades of my existence took me to places where happiness and joy were not the ordinary way of life for me. But at the same time these were the motivating forces behind my determination to be blessed with the life God has given to me now. Having been a daughter, a mother, a woman, a minister, a counselor and a friend, I have FINALLY come back to my most important self… a child of the Most High God.

I dare to hope that you will discover something in you that helps you to make the difference in whatever moment you live right now, even if it doesn't look or feel good. My prayer is that you dare to take the journey back to yourself.

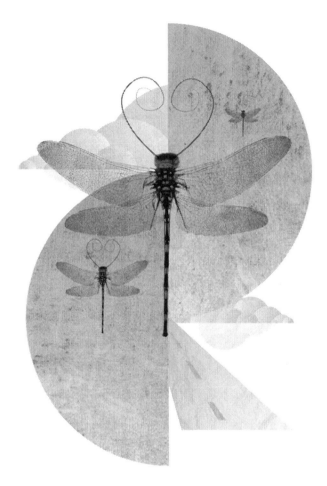

"My son, hear the instruction of your father and do not
forsake the law of your mother"
Proverbs 1:8

CHAPTER 1

Ohio

I was 7 and I was always dressed sharp. My mom made sure of that. This day was no exception. I wore a burnt orange and black plaid skirt and jacket with a black blouse and black patent leather shoes, I also had a black patent leather purse to match. Driving in the car, my mom is making sure I understand exactly how to use the telephone and what to do when making a collect call. She makes sure I know not to talk to anyone but the pilot and the stewardesses. She explains what will happen once I reach the plane and tells me not to be afraid. Then I see the airport. The planes are huge, I can't imagine how in the world they are going to ever fit on the freeway to drive me to my daddy. Inside the airport there are so many people I cling tightly to my mom's hand for fear that she'll lose me in the crowd if I should let go. We walk onto the plane straight to the stewardess, my mom says, "My name is Carolyn and this is Zina, she is my only daughter and she's headed to Ohio to visit her dad, Wali Bahar. I can pay you extra if you can make sure that she doesn't have any problem on this flight. This is her first trip by plane." The stewardess cheerfully accepts responsibility of me but refuses the tip. My mom lets her know that in my suitcase there is piece of paper with all our information right on top of my clothes. I tell my mom don't worry I'll be fine. Reluctant and full of tears my mom leaves the plane. I look for her in the window but I don't see her. I'm not afraid though, I just wait patiently for my plane to drive me to my daddy. Looking back, it's right here that my journey to becoming an adult takes shape. Being old enough to take this trip all alone, I'm certain that this is what growing up must be all about. The stewardess seats me close by her station so she can check on me periodically. After getting me situated, she goes about her normal duties.

The plane is big and I feel like a munchkin in my seat. But my big girl, grown up clothes provide me with the necessary confidence to know I can pull this off. I'm not scared. My grandmother taught me about God and how He will always protect me when I'm afraid. My grandmother, Willie Zell (lovingly called, Piggy) was never afraid of anything. God was ALWAYS the head of her house...ever since before I was even born. She believed God could solve ANY problem and that He was the "Great I' AM" & that He would never leave her or forsake her. He was her Lord and Savior. He could be everywhere, see everything and knew everything before it even happened. I believed this "I AM" God would do the same thing for me. Because of this, I knew I didn't have to fear any evil and that no harm would come to me. Back on the plane, my stewardess comes by to make sure my seat belt is buckled tight. I wonder why it is taking so long for the plane to go. What are we waiting for? I haven't seen my daddy in a whole lot of days and I can't wait any longer. I smile at the thought that soon he'll be hugging me and calling me his little "sweetie pie" all summer long. I hear my stewardess tell her friend, "it's time". Her friend goes to the front of the plane takes down a small microphone and begins to explain "*safety procedures*". I guess planes are so big you have to have things like "*oxygen mask*" and "*emergency exits*" so if you get in an accident on the freeway, it won't be so bad. Just before she finishes, I hear a loud noise. It's the engine. I think, "Man, it sure is loud". My stewardess and all of her friends check each passenger to make sure they're buckled in too. My stewardess takes her seat next to me. I sure am glad I get to ride next to her. This plan engine is so loud, I feel a little shaky. As we pull down the runway, I watch the airport get further and further away. We turn around, straighten up, and then the plane starts to speed. I ask my stewardess why we're going so fast. She tells me it's because the plane has to build up enough power so when it leaves the ground it can stay up in the air. This is when things become too much for me to handle. "Why do we have to leave the ground to get to the freeway?" "I don't want to leave the ground. I don't want to be in the air." As the plane begins to go up, tears start to stream down my face. I'm terrified, but I promised I'd be a big girl, I can't let my stewardess, and all these people see that I'm not. I can't let her know I'm scared and I want get off this big thing. I wonder, to myself, if the "I AM" God that Piggy talks about all the time, knew about this. If He did know, did He tell my mom and forget to tell me? I'm not feeling so much like a big girl anymore. I'm able to conceal my terror until I see the city I've lived in all my life become teeny, tiny houses and swimming pools. Normal cars look like little toys. Then my city becomes a funny shaped square. I start to see other little squares around it. It all turns into a blur of lights that began to look like stars as the sun begins to set. Now I think, maybe there has been a mistake. I don't know these people. My mom didn't know these people. These people could be kidnapping me. All that I knew about how to make a collect call would not help me now. I began to cry uncontrollably, out loud. I didn't know what else to do. I felt helpless and alone. Just then, my faith seemed as small as the town I once lived in. Piggy always said if I was ever alone & in trouble, I could talk to God. This felt like big trouble so I began to talk to God and tell Him how scared I was. Then...

my stewardess asked me what was wrong. When I told her I was afraid of being kidnapped, she asked if the pilot himself told me he would take me straight to my daddy would I believe him and feel better. She took my seat belt off, gently tugged at my hand, and led me into the cockpit. There I was with the pilot and the Co-pilot. I can't describe how beautiful the world looked through the front of that cockpit window. The world was gone and what was left was a big, beautiful blue sky with big puffy white clouds. We glided so smooth through the air and everything felt quiet and still. I remember thinking "this must be what heaven looked like". My astonishment will never leave me. The pilot spoke in a strong but authoritative tone. (Just like my daddy.) He said "what's wrong Zina, are you a little afraid?" He knew my name. Out of all the people on the plane, the pilot knew my name. I felt special. I was important. I was a BIG GIRL! We talked for a long time, me and *my* pilot. He explained everything he had to do to fly the plane, and what would happen once it landed. He told me there was nothing for me to be afraid of and that he would get me to my daddy "A.S.A.P." Now I didn't know exactly what that meant but I was sure it meant pretty fast. I thanked him for taking time to make me feel comfortable, then told him I was ready to go back to my seat. He reached to call my stewardess, I assured him that I could make back on my own. I don't remember much else about the plane ride except that the food was good, the movie was funny, and that sleeping was not a problem. When I woke up, I saw those funny squares again. Thinking I was back home, I ask my stewardess, "wasn't my daddy there for me, why am I going back home?" She told me we were about to land in Ohio and that my daddy should be there waiting for me. I could hardly wait. I ran to the bathroom to make sure I look really pretty for him. Being sure that I was, I got back to my seat and waited patiently for the plane to land. Upon exiting the plane, my stewardess took me by the hand and led me through the crowd to an open space where I could be seen. Soon I saw him and he was fine. My father was the most handsome man I knew and there would never be anybody who could take his place. I was lucky, my mom never talked bad about him. She allowed me to grow up and get to know him for myself. She never tried to introduce me to her "Ex-Husband", instead...she let me know my daddy!I saw him standing there in his handsome steel gray suit. He had on a starch white shirt, black and gray pattern tie, and mirror shined black shoes. I could hardly move fast enough. Snatching away from my new friend, as though she meant nothing, I ran and jumped into my daddy's arms. Hugging him so tight, I could smell his cologne. He always smelled so good to me. The smell of my dad would make its way up my nose, linger around in my head, then live in my mental and emotional memories for many a day. Sometime when he wasn't around I'd just sit on the floor in the middle of his closet and smell his suites. When I was sad, that would make me happy. When I was mad, that would make me glad. When done with our hellos I looked around for my stepmother and my two baby sisters Wanda & Alicia. He said they were home waiting for me with Deena. Deena was dad's new wife. He met and married her in LA but they moved to Santa Barbara not long after that. That's where I met her. She was really young and pretty. Being a Muslim, she always wore a head covering, tunic and long skirt. She made her own clothes. She made mine too since I didn't have anything to wear to the Mosque. Even though she was young, Deena tried to be a good step-mother. During our first meeting she was quiet and soft spoken, not like mom. She seemed to be very aware of my dad's every need, from the clothes being ironed with strong creases to making sure he had dinner made special for him. She would even serve him steak even when we had bean soup. I didn't like how she was so fussy over him. My mom wasn't like that. Whatever she cooked is what EVERYBODY ate. When I was 7, mom met and married David. He wasn't anywhere near as handsome as my daddy. He had a roughness about his look that I just didn't like. But he didn't care that I didn't like him. He adored me and always treated me like his own daughter. He never hesitated to tell people how proud of me he was. But that didn't matter to me. For me, he would NEVER measure up to my daddy! My mom never made a fuss over him and he loved my mom anyway. I made a decision that I would never fuss over a man the way that Deena did. I felt like she was trying to prove to him

17

that she was better than my mom and that she could take care of him better than her. Even though she was not my mom, I figured I would have to be nice to her because she was the mother of my two sisters. I decided that being a good big sister was more important than giving my new step mom a hard time. Wanda was born in Santa Barbara before they moved to Ohio. Alicia was born a few months before I arrived. Being an only child at home with my mom, I looked forward to being the older sister at home with my dad. I often fantasized about the times when we would all be older and I'd be able to share with my two younger siblings all the wicked ways of the world to be cautious of. Riding back to the house, I told my dad all about my plane trip and how well they took care of me. He said "those whitey's know they better had of taken care of his baby or he would have to take care of them." I didn't know why he didn't like white people, I just thought that maybe they treated him really mean before.

Being in Ohio seemed so different than being in California. The trees seemed so big and so beautiful. They all seemed to sway in the same direction. Even the streets seemed wider. It took us a long time to reach the house but I enjoyed the view and the smell of my dad's cologne all the way. We turned onto this beautiful tree lined street, with manicured lawns. The houses seemed enormous. We pulled into the driveway of the biggest, most beautiful, brick house I'd ever seen. "Is this your house daddy?" I gasped. "No baby, this is our house. When you come to me every summer, just know that you are at home." When we walked in, my dad hung my coat near the stairs then I saw Wanda. She had gotten so big, I couldn't believe it. I had just seen her the year before. She was almost as tall as me. She had a little round head with cute pig tales all over, big round eyes and a bright smile. She ran to give me a big hug. With hellos done, I ask "where is our new little sister?" "Over there" she replied. Then I saw Alicia. She was sitting in her walker in the living room. Even though she had not seen me before, she seemed to recognize me. I just broke into side splitting laughter because she looked just like me. I had never experienced anything like that before. She had a big round head with little tight eyes and chubby cheeks. Her head was covered with cute, thick, black curls all over. She looked just like all of the baby pictures of me I had seen so far. If I weren't me, I would have thought she was me. It was a trip.

The summer went by really fast. I made new friends and got to know my little sisters. It was fun dressing up in pantaloons, tunics, and head dresses. My father being Muslim, at the Mosque I got to experience a whole new religion. Looking back now, I believed that the NOI (Nation of Islam) was an organization that empowered Black people to know their significance. According to my young minds understanding, they seemed to be against the "White Man" controlling their life and destiny. Today, I know that there is much more to it than that. They taught that Blacks were "the original human being" and they adopted many of the Eastern Muslim traditions from the Holy Koran (their Bible). They also studied the "Five Pillars of Islam", 1) Faith in the oneness of God; 2) daily prayers; 3) concern for the needy; 4) self-purification thru fasting and 5) pilgrimage to Mecca. They coupled a lot of that with the practices of Black Power, but not in the same way as the Black Panthers. The

Black Panthers were a revolutionary socialist organization active in the the US during the late 60's thru the mid 70's. Their core practice was its "armed citizens" patrol that monitored the behavior of police officers and challenged police brutality. I didn't so much like how all the women and girls were separated from the men and boys, I didn't understand why the rules were so different between the sexes, & I didn't like that the boys were taught cool drills and the girls taught about natural blush by pinching our cheeks. Being a young Muslim girl, I was dressed covered from head to toe. It was not appropriate for girls to show their bodies to be gawked at. I didn't like this custom because I was used to dressing in shorts & halter tops during the summer, but I had to go along with the rules. We were treated so differently and it seemed that the boys had all the fun with more stuff to do. The only things the girls were taught were task needed for taking care of a husband and family. But the Muslim Sisters were so nice to me that I still enjoyed it all. Being a Muslim wasn't so bad. Deena was young, pretty and slim, and she was always around. She didn't have to work so much like my mom. Mom had been working in the Aerospace industry all my life. She took a job at Ampex, after divorcing my father. When she was younger, she was so dependent on my father (& grandmother) that she was determined not to ever need anyone's help again. Also, because of her doing without so much as a child, she was determined to give me the best of everything. With this belief system firmly in place, she set out to make her own money. As a result, she worked constantly, 13 & 14 hour days and 6 & 7 days a week. This left me in the care of my grandmother most days. Although my grandmother loved me very much and took excellent care of me, she wasn't my mom. Spending so much time with my grandmother, it felt like my two aunties (who were only 10 and 13 years old) were my big sisters (and I always wanted an older sister or brother). I liked laying around and making Deena laugh. But I didn't like the way she made me eat. My sisters and I always had chicken and we always had to eat in the kitchen. We could not have anything to drink with our dinner, only after our food was completely finished could we have anything to drink. My dad would have his dinner separate. Coming home late from work, we'd already be done. He always had to have his dinner freshly cooked and set on a TV tray just before he walked in, it was usually steak. Because it had to be freshly cooked, Deena would have to get up from bed and cook for him in the middle of the night. She didn't want me to stay up and wait for him but I did anyway. Soon the summer was over, it was time for me to go home, even though I didn't want to.

I went to visit my dad every summer from 1967 to 1976. Many things happened over these summers as I continued to grow into a young girl. One year when I got to Ohio my father drove all of us to Mississippi to visit his mother, she sure was mean. The streets were dirt roads and there were no sidewalks. All the houses looked small but they had big porches. At the end of our block was a park. The park was the center and meeting place for our small town. It had a big, dusty baseball diamond in the middle, with swings and slides on the side. Next to the swings was a shed that sold ice cream and soda pop. There was not much else to do in Mississippi except catch fire-flies. A few days after we got there my dad got into a fight with some old disgusting drunk man at the park. I'm not sure who won because my dad told my uncle Scott to take me back to the house. I didn't see my dad for weeks after that. He must have lost the fight because I found out later he went back to Ohio to recuperate and that he would send for us soon. I had to stay with my mean old grandmother for almost the whole summer that year. I was miserable. Every day she would make me do chores around the house. Since my sisters were afraid of dogs, I would have to stay outside with her two dogs until my stepmom got in from work. I cried ever day for my dad. I didn't travel to stay with her, I came to visit my dad. And since I wasn't with him, I wanted to go home. I promised myself that if I ever got out of Mississippi, I'd never go back. And I never did! When my father did show back up Deena was really angry, and at the time I didn't know why. We had everything we needed, my father made sure she had a job while we were there so we wouldn't need anything. AND...He did come back for us. When we got back to Ohio, there was brand new furniture in the living room and dining room. When Deena saw it, she didn't even seem happy. If my husband had done that for me I would have been very excited, but she wasn't. We were not allowed to sit on the furniture even though it was covered with plastic. As I got older there seem to be more and more for me to do for my younger sisters. Deena and my dad didn't seem to talk at all. He was hardly ever there. I just figured that his job must have changed his work hours. One year I was in Ohio and it seemed that everything my dad did was wrong because Deena would fuss about his every move. One night after a really big argument in their bedroom, my dad stormed out of the room and slammed the door. As he was headed out of the door, Deena came out and said "take your daughter with you. She is here to visit you not me." I didn't know why Deena wanted him to take me to work with him, but if he would have me I would sure like to go. He turned to face Deena and simply said "NO PROBLEM", I'd never seen my dad in so much rage. He was almost unrecognizable to me. But when he turned to me his whole face seemed to change...to transform. He looked at me and said "come on baby, you wanna go with daddy." Leaving Akron headed to Youngstown, my daddy told me about the lady he had to take care of.

Her husband was his friend and had died. My daddy told me the story of how his friend was on his death bed & asked my daddy to take care of his wife and kids, my dad promised him he would. I didn't know it then but that was not the truth and before the next summer Deena and my two precious baby sisters moved to LA. I thought that was just fine, I needed them close to me as they grew up anyway so if they had life questions they could just ask. My mom already had my little brother Jack who was only three at the time. Now I had three siblings to look after and it was a good thing that they were all in the same state.

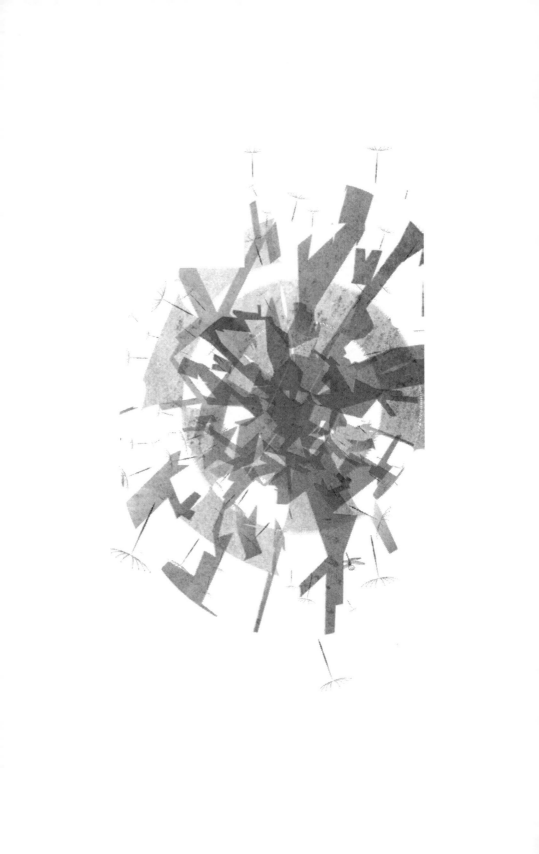

"So I am not exalted above measure, I received a thorn in my flesh. I asked the Lord to remove it and he said my grace is sufficient, for my strength is made perfect in your weakness"
II Cor. 12:7-9

CHAPTER 2

Shattered Dreams

In 1974, we were living on Wilton Place in Hawthorne, California and it was a really cool neighborhood. The city was preparing for a new freeway that would run down the middle of our neighborhood. The city was buying up all the property in the area. Once the houses were empty they would tear them down and clear the land. It was really sad because all my friends were moving away and where there was once a nice neighborhood with manicured lawns on tree lined streets, there was now just vacant lots. You could see almost up to Western which was four blocks and up the hill away. In the last block there was a cul-de-sac, just before the hill. The city had bought those houses and they were vacant but still standing. It was in one of these houses that I was raped by some old man that I didn't know. As I was headed to school I was approached by a man in his mid to late 30's. He asked if I wanted a ride to school and I said no. When he didn't succeed to get me in his car, he proceeded on his way. When I arrived to the next block, I saw him again and he stopped. He asked if I were sure about not taking the ride, I declined again. For some reason, I didn't think anything about seeing him twice on the block. I just figured he was headed back out of the neighborhood. To my surprise, he came from one of the houses on the next block by foot. He walked right up to me and put a knife to my throat and told me don't scream. He took me into one of the houses and tied me up. I couldn't believe what was happening to me. It seemed like a nightmare, like I was watching a scary movie. I was in such a state of shock that I began to question him as to what he intended to do with me. When he said "you know what's about to happen", I was sincerely clueless. After all, I was just a kid, who would want a little girl like me. He ripped the cord from some old venetian blinds still hanging on the window. He used it to tie my hands behind my back. He took off my pants and underwear and begin to try and penetrate me. He didn't seem to get the desired response so he kept trying. It seemed like we were there for hours. When he was done, he said "you can't really call it rape because I couldn't get in anyway". I felt violated for a second time. What did he mean by this statement. Was he trying to say I couldn't even be raped successfully. As strange as it seems, this was a blow to my ego because I already felt like I couldn't do anything right. Now here I was being told by a rapist that I couldn't even be raped right. What was that about! He told me to count to 100 before getting dressed. I did and then...I went onto school anyway. Headed to Henry Clay Jr. High, I held a straight face until I got there. I found my best friend Stephanie and told her what had happened. It must have been around April because she thought it was an April fool's joke. When she realized I was telling the truth she cried with me in the bathroom until the nurse arrived. I didn't want to tell the nurse my story so she took me to the principal, who I certainly wasn't going to talk to. That's when they called my mom. I was so embarrassed, I just wanted to put the whole thing behind me and forget about it. But she called the police and I had to tell them. They took me to the doctor and I had to tell them. Then I had to take an officer to the scene and take them step by step through what had happened. Then they had to write it down so I had to tell another officer while she hand wrote the report. Lastly, I had to give a description to another officer. By then I was so disgusted with telling the whole story that I just shut down. When I gave the description to the police artist, the picture didn't look like the guy but I lied and said it did. I didn't want to tell the story anymore and sure didn't want to see his face in my mind anymore. I crawled inside myself and I was determined to stay in there. My precious innocence had been stolen, I had no more virtue to protect, and my self-esteem was at the lowest possible place. I had concluded that outside my imagination was no safe place and I would not exist outside myself any longer. This whole God idea, that my grandmother had was for the birds, He didn't hear my prayers, didn't send angels to protect me and certainly wasn't anyone I wanted to call "Father". If my father had been there, this surely would never have happened. He would surely have protected me or at least took care of that old man that stole my future. I was only 13 and I was still a virgin. He stole my innocence from me and it would be gone forever. I don't remember much about that summer except thinking that I could sleep with anybody I wanted to because I didn't have any virtue I needed to protect anymore (I did) and that I didn't see my father that year. I was numb but decided to bury that incident as deep inside myself that I could find and never bring it up again. Thinking I had put that time far behind me, I looked forward to the new school year and all the new experiences being in high school would bring.

It was the fall of 1974, and I was starting my first year at Washington High school. Because I was in modern dance at Henry Clay, the dance instructor already knew me. Mrs. Jackson insisted I join the modern dance troupe in addition to the class. One day we were in the auditorium practicing for the school holiday play. There was one number when the choir would sing to the music of the band while we danced. I noticed the drummer who was dark chocolate fine. I took office worker as an elective and while there took advantage of my access to student information files. I found out his name was Gregory Samuels, I got his address, phone number, and his schedule of classes. I knew he was on the football team and played in the band. Using the information from all my investigations, I made sure I showed up anywhere I thought he'd be. I became his friend and then made an attempt to get him to see me as more than that. I even tried to get him to teach me to play the drums. When that didn't work, I became very forward. I made it known that I had a crush and that I would not go away until he made me his girlfriend. He was so sweet, and as gently as he could, he let me know that he only saw me as a friend and he didn't want to see me hurt. I went home and told my mother that I had a crush on a boy who didn't like me and I didn't know what to do. She told me to ignore that, just be his friend, and one day he would come around. She also told me that when he did come around to let him know that he missed his chanced. We remained only friends throughout that year, then he graduated. I was excited anyway because I was going to see my dad, who had moved to Chicago.

In the summer of 1975 I got to visit my dad and his new wife Halimah. She was Minister Elijah Muhummad's niece (he was the leader of the Nation of Islam). I had missed my dad so much. It was the first time I had skipped a summer since 1967. I knew about his new family and it was important to me that I get out there as soon as possible so my new siblings could get to know me. I had a responsibility you know. Halimah already had two sons, Akbar and Sabir, but she had my brother Sadeem the year before and had just had my youngest brother Amir a few months before I arrived. I felt so much like the big sister and it was so cool. They had been given a new home as a wedding present. This was no ordinary house. It was a huge brick house and it was located right in the middle of an area called Pill Hill. There were a lot of doctors who owned homes in this area. This house was beautiful. When you walk in there was a huge chandelier ball that hung from a really high ceiling, red carpeted stairs going up and brown and beige carpet going down. To my left was the living room that had red carpet throughout, a white baby grand piano, white antique furniture, ceiling to floor mirrors on one wall and ceiling to floor windows on the front wall. These windows were not paneled, they were four full picture windows that made up the front wall of the house. Around the corner from the living room was the dining room on the same red carpet, there sat in all its majesty was an antique, white stained wood, six chair dining room table, regally positioned in front of an identical china closet. I felt like I was in some royal palace, everything was so big, so grand, and so elegant. Upstairs were three bedrooms, my two younger brothers shared a room and the two older ones shared the other room. Halimah shared a room with my dad in the middle. Downstairs was a den with a pool table and a sitting room with white leather furniture. I created my own room in the basement and you could not tell me that I was not in heaven. Until I met "*him*", Theodore Johnson Brickman Jr. He was the finest boy on the block and I was gonna marry him and have all his children. It was a summer of love and innocence. There was a lot of laughter that summer. I teased my dad about being so serious and about the other kids on the block being afraid of him. I made good friends, while he continued to try keep them all afraid of him. My brothers and I were very close. Halimah would do facials with me late at night. You know it's funny because she would get up in the middle of the night to make my dad steaks too, just like Deena, I never got that. I did make up my mind that my husband would eat whatever my kids ate and he would eat it at dinner time or fix it himself. It's funny how a belief system sets up shop in the subconscious. We react to it for the rest of our lives never knowing why or where it even came from. My dad tried his best to keep me the naive little girl he could tell any story to and I'd believe. But I was growing up, against his will even. I don't know if he knew about the rape, I wasn't going to tell him, but it did change me. I was not a little girl anymore, that man made me a woman. All the curiosity that innocence brings was gone now. The questions I had about sex had changed. I no longer dreamed of how my 1st time would be. Now I only wanted to know what would make an old man desire a child. What was so big about sex that would drive a man to steal the innocence of a child. These things didn't matter as much because now I was a woman and I needed to make decisions for myself. Besides, I couldn't go around listening to my daddy when my future husband had a much different concept. Theodore Brickman was the 1st person I'd ever seen stand up to my dad. It was frightening and exhilarating at the same time. It was the best summer vacation I'd had with my dad ever. Theodore made it everything it had never been before. He was going to the 12th grade and he was more mature than any other boy I had been with. That made me feel more mature. Man, I just knew I'd be in love with him forever.

It was the end to another summer and I was very sad. Not only did I have to leave my dad, Halimah, my brothers and new friends but I had to leave Theodore Brickman. I didn't think I would survive the separation. The night before I was to leave, Theodore Brickman came to the basement window, as he had done so often during the summer, I snuck out of the back door. We walked his dog down the alley for blocks and talked. We talked about our future. He'd finish his last year in high school and apply for one of the Los Angeles universities. He was a straight "A" student so there would be no problems. I'd continue my schooling and once I'd graduated we'd get married. During this year we'd write every day and call once a week. He promised me we'd be okay. As the sun began to rise, I knew my family would be waking and I'd better get in. We said our good-byes and in tears I turned and walked away.

Back in Los Angeles, it was the fall of 1975 and I was warming up for dance practiced. I was sitting in a split with my back to the door. My girlfriend was facing me when she said, "oh my, who is that?" I turned to see Gregory in the doorway. I was so excited to see him, I jumped up and gave him a big hug. He was looking for one of the girls who was not there yet. We caught up on what had been happening for the past summer. After talking for a minute, I remembered what my mom had said. I told him it was nice seeing him again and that I had to get back to practice. He said OK and reminded me that he was still available for those drum lessons. With a coy smile I whispered to him, "sorry but you missed your chance." With that, I simply went back to my stretching and never looked back. That felt good.

I wrote Theodore every day and called much too often for my mother's taste. I went on about my life with the plan Theodore and I talked about. Soon his letters began to slow down. I'd call and he would not be home. I mailed three letters in a row and did not receive a response. My relationship was over. I couldn't believe it, we were through. I cried a lot then decided to move on. Only a few months had passed but you could never have told me that then. My precious time with Theodore seemed like eons of millenniums before. It's strange how time moves so slowly when you're young but the same 24 hour days seem to speed by fast enough to take your breath away when you're older.

Living on Wilton Place was a family down the street called, The Andersons. There were a lot of them and they were wild. My mom didn't want me to associate with any of them. But they seemed so cool. I became friends with Robin who was about my age. Every day she would come down to my house and we'd go to the park at the end of the block. One day she told me about a boy she used to go with, Antonio

Giovanni. He was an Italian boy she knew from somewhere, I don't know where, but she was crazy about Antonio. Robin always talked about what her life was going to be like when she got Antonio back. She was going have his baby and he would marry her. It sounded a lot like how I felt about Theodore. So we'd compare stories about our future husbands and laugh. One day she called me and told me to come outside, she had a surprise for me. When I got out there she was walking up the street with this really cute boy, I knew it had to be Antonio. She introduced us and we talked for a little while. It was almost time for dinner and I had to go in. I told Antonio it was nice to meet him, winked at Robin and went inside. I didn't think too much about Antonio after that, I just hoped that Robin's plan would work. A couple of months after that, I came home from choir rehearsal and my mom told me that some white boy had come to see me. I couldn't imagine who that could be. I hadn't met any white boys and if I had, I certainly didn't give my number or address to anyone. I didn't think anything of it. A couple of hours later the doorbell rang and it was Antonio. He was standing there with a big bouquet of flowers. He said, "Zina, I'd like it very much if you would consider going to the show with me." I thanked him for the flowers, told him I was flattered, but that I would not be able to accept his invitation. I reminded him that Robin was still very much in love with him and that it would feel like a betrayal for me to go out with him. He insisted I take the flowers, told me he understood and gave me his number, in case I changed my mind. When he left, I was putting the flowers in water when I heard shouting outside. I went to see what was going on and Robin's whole family was outside cursing me for being a back stabber. It hurt me to know my friend would think I would go behind her back and try to steal her boyfriend. I was a more loyal friend than that. But she would not even let me explain. My attempts to explain were met with rage and threats to my life. I thought me and Robin were friends, I couldn't believe she would not even hear my side. After being harassed at home and school for several weeks doing nothing, I decided to be harassed for doing something. I stopped refusing Antonio's attempts to see me and we began to date. My mother

41

refused to let me fight her and my own rage was bubbling over because I was not allowed to defend my mother and my brother from the harassment and threats. It became too much for my mother to deal with. One day we were at my grandmother's house. A call came from my cousin who lived down the street from us. She told us to come home immediately, that our house lights were on and the doors were open. When we walked in there were broken windows and my bedroom had been ransacked. My mother was so hurt and angry that we packed and moved that night. I did not return to school. One week later, to the day, I was on a plane to Chicago to live with my dad. It was January 1976 and it was snowing. Some little witch with a bigger family than me had run my family out of our home, ran me away from my school, and had actually run me out of town. I was pissed and humiliated. This would never happen to me again. If anyone had a problem with something I did they would either have to confront it or fight it out right there. There would be no more situations that would be left to linger for months on end. NEVER AGAIN! It's funny how we make decisions as children and think things will remain that way forever.

A lot had happened since that first plane ride to Ohio. I had blossomed into a young woman with quite a few issues. But I believed myself to be a full woman just the same. You couldn't tell me that I was still a child, scarred by a rape I couldn't prevent, hurt by a boy who stopped returning my calls and humiliated by a girl and her family that ran me out of town. In my mind I was a woman and no one could tell me different.

"He who keeps instruction is in the way of life, but he who refuses correction goes astray"
Proverbs 10:17

CHAPTER 3

Chicago

It was the beginning of winter and I was back in Chicago, faced with a new situation. I had to face Theodore and his anger about Antonio. I was there for a week before I built up enough courage to go down the street and face him. It seemed an entire lifetime had passed since that day he finally called. He apologized for not calling sooner and for not responding to my letters. He told me he was trying to ace all his mid-terms so he would increase his chances for getting into one of the LA colleges. He was still following the plan. But it had been so long since I had heard from him. Between him not calling and Robin giving me constant grief, I just broke to Antonio's attempts to get my attention. When I told Theodore that day, he screamed in horror that I had betrayed him. He sobbed like a baby, the phone hit the wall, and I listened to him have this fit for about 30 minutes. It was painful but it was too late. I was already involved with Antonio. We were planning our future, I was committed and I would not go back on that. Through tears and sobs and slobs I had to whisper to him, "I'm sorry but you missed your chance." Now here I was thrust back to Chicago. There was no way that Antonio and I would be able to maintain a long distance relationship for the next two years. I had to face Theodore and I wanted to get it over with. Early one morning, when I knew his parents had left for work, I put on one of Halimah's fur coats and I headed down the street. I managed to get my brother's to keep my presence quiet, so he didn't know I was there. Standing there, I ranged the bell, he answered the door. It was as if a big gust of wind knocked him off his feet when he saw me. His mouth dropped and he didn't say a word. Finally, I said "well are you going to let me in or do I have stand out here in the cold." He opened the door and grabbed me, he held me so tight, I couldn't breathe. He asked me what I was doing in Chicago, I told him that my mom and I were having some problems and she thought it best that I finish high school with my dad. He asked me what had happened with Antonio, I simply said it was over and that it had been over for a long time. Standing there in that moment, it felt like we could just pick up from where we had left off last summer. We didn't know how things had really changed and how they would never be the same.

Not long after I returned to Chicago, it snowed for the first time since I had been there. I had never seen snow, so for me it was awesome. It was late one night and I slept in the living room because the carpet was soft and everyone had said it would snow soon and I wanted to see it as soon as it happened. I peeked out the big picture window and it was there. Everything was so beautiful, there was a solid white blanket over everything outside. Soft flakes were falling so gently it seemed as if they were falling in slow motion. It was so pure and gentle. It had been untouched. There were no footprints, no tire tracks, no dirt and everything was white. It was as if God had covered the world with a blanket. I felt His presence and it felt safe. It wasn't like my grandmother's God, it was God personal to me. This personal God was much more kind and patient than the jealous, punishing God my grandmother taught me about. For one split second I knew and understood God's meaning of love. There was a peace I couldn't describe that came with that first snow…I had to touch it. My dad had told me that if it should snow and he wasn't around, I should not play in it because I didn't have the proper clothing. I knew if I wanted to play in it, I should do it right then or he wouldn't let me. I went to my room and dressed as warm as I could. I put on two pairs of pants, two shirts, a sweat shirt, a sweater and a jacket. I put on a beanie hat and a big coat and snuck out of the back door. I tried to tiptoe to the back yard but the snow was too deep. I stumbled and stammered until I finally made it to the back. I picked up a handful of snow and rubbed my face in it. I romped and stomped and played. I laid down to make an angel, I laughed and giggled. I was truly a child again, innocent, it was fun. I knew that I should probably get back in before I got caught so I headed for the back door. When I reached for the door, I couldn't bend my fingers. In my excitement, I forgot that I needed gloves. My fingers were froze. I couldn't let my father catch me outside, I needed to figure a way to get inside. Using both hands, I managed to turn the knob, come in, close the door and get mostly undressed, but my hands were throbbing. The only thing I knew to do was run hot water on them so that they would thaw out, but instead they began to burn. I didn't know that you should use cold water for frost bite. After doing that I thought if I go to sleep, when I woke up it would be better. When I got up the next morning my hands were in so much pain I couldn't keep it secret anymore. I couldn't even put my hands down by my side. I had to walk around with my hands above my head so they wouldn't throb. Although angry, my dad said I look so ridiculous it was punishment enough for me to walk around like that. He took me to the doctor, who said there was no serious damage, gave me some cream, and sent me home to be ridiculed by everybody else in the family and neighborhood.

Frost bite aside, living in Chicago was a trip. My dad said it was time for me to choose a high school to attend. CVS High School was the closest to home but Theodore said there were too many guys there so I choose Kenwood Academy. It was in Hyde Park, close to where Halimah worked. My father had long since changed his name from Bobby Moorhead to Wali Bahar, he said Moorhead was the slave name the White man gave him. Before enrolling me in high school he decided he would change my name to Zanell Bahar so I wouldn't have a slave name either. It's funny to me today how I thought my dad to be so powerful. In my mind he could do anything with no questions asked. I never gave a second thought to the name change, it wasn't even legal. He just changed my name, took me to school and enrolled me under this alias, and no one ever questioned it. Kenwood was cool, the entire school was in one humongous building, even the swimming pool. I had never been in a school like that. Apparently, all the schools in the snow states were like that. It prevented the students from having to travel from building to building in the snow. Everyone seemed to be mixed with two or more races there. I didn't see too many people who were all one race. Most of the boys were fine and most of the girls were snobs. I didn't fit into either of those categories, I wasn't fine or a snob, so I felt sort out place until people found out I was from California. As fascinated as I was about being in Chicago, with all of its beautiful snow, the people there were fascinated about California, with all of its sun and movie stars. I was constantly asked the question of what stars I had seen walking down the streets of LA, what a joke. There were no after school clubs in this school and I didn't like that. I had no place to dance and no school play to perform in. I would do modern dance in the hallway by the gym alone. Every so often some people would gather around and watch me but it was very unfulfilling. I enrolled in the drama class just for a creative outlet. It didn't take long for me to develop a knack for acting, but still there was no school play so it was also very unfulfilling. It was not very fulfilling but it did allow me a forum to become friends with some of the kids there. I was not a leader I was a follower, and I did not know how to create an avenue for my creative expression. I resented my mother for sending me away against my will, and now not only did I look like a fool in the eyes of those I left in California, but I also would never dance again, and it was all her fault. She never even believed I could make a living as a dancer. She always thought I needed to get good grades, go to college, get a job, make average money, pay taxes and retire to being alone, miserable, and bitter until my death. And now she had succeeded in making sure I would never fulfill my dream to dance and I'd live my life like she had, an unhappy workaholic. She had won! I found out later that there were no clubs because these people went out and did full-fledged projects on their own. They were creative enough not to need the guidance of the school, they were putting on plays, writing concerts, performing creative dances, modeling, acting and anything else they wanted to do, all on their own. That was amazing to me, I had never seen people so young creating their own venues for expression, and I had never had such independence, freedom, or initiative.

Things were beginning to take on a routine at home. I was adjusting to living in Chicago and being raised in a Muslim family, even though I continued to go to different churches. I especially enjoyed the churches that played tambourines, shouted with the Holy Ghost, hooped and hollered. It was like being back home. I was still with Theodore but things were strained. He had a hard time accepting that I had been with anyone other than him. He began to bring up constant reminders that I could not be trusted, throwing the past in my face, and not treating me very nice. I believed he had a right to feel the way he did, because I was the one who stopped following the plan. I believed I deserved to be treated that way because I didn't have any faith in him and I didn't remain true. Ever since the rape I didn't put much value in my worth. My self-esteem was zero. It was easy to treat me like crap because I felt like crap anyway. I took his verbal abuse for as long as I could. Finally I said, hey if you can't get over the past to be with me now, then I guess it must be over. This started a new cycle of breaking up and getting back together. Once I'd had enough, I broke up with him for good. It was very painful but I stood my ground. For the next couple of months, I tried to date other guys but anyone who came to my house was harassed by

Theodore. Most of them had to catch the bus, and they had to pass his house first to get to mine. He would sit on his porch and ask every teenage guy if he was coming to see me. If the answer was yes, he beat them up and they would not come back. So I couldn't have anyone, while he continued to date whomever he chose. I met one guy who had a car. I told him about Theodore and he said he wasn't worried. One day he came over to visit. We were in the den listening to music for a long time. When he was leaving, I walked him to the driveway to make sure Theodore wouldn't bother him. When he was safely in his car I went back inside. A few hours later, my doorbell rang, it was Theodore. He was standing there playing with this antenna. Before I could ask what he wanted, the phone rang. I left Theodore at the door to answer the phone, it was the guy. He told me that someone had broken into his car, cracked up his sunglasses, burnt his graduation tassel, and took his CB antenna. He said if I knew who it was, to get his antenna back and let them know that he carried a gun and didn't mind using it. I told him that I would retrieve his antenna and if he didn't have the guts to deliver the message in person then he didn't have enough courage for me to be dealing with. When I got back to the door, Theodore was laughing in my face. He said if my boyfriend wanted his antenna back he would have to come get it himself. Theodore told me that he was standing outside with the antenna when my boyfriend came out and that the punk was too chicken shit to ask for it back. I asked him did he want to get back with me and he said no. I told him if he didn't want me anymore then stop running everybody else away. I see now that I had no self-worth, I would have taken him back because I felt like a rag doll to be used by whoever. He told me that he did want to but he couldn't get rid of the pictures of me with someone else in his mind. He said he was angry with me and that he wanted to pay me back for the hurt that I had caused him. He said he loved me and always would and that he wanted to try once more. I told him he would always have a place in my heart and that no one else could ever be my first love. I told him that I wished things could be different but they weren't. I told him I could be his friend, try not to throw a lot in his face, but that we had missed the chance to keep this as special as it had always been. Too much had happened, it was too late. Then I went inside, closed the door, and cried myself to sleep.

I met Rhonda Skinner and she became my best friend. Her father was an Alderman and mother had died before I met her. She was the oldest girl in her family too. She had three younger sisters and two older brothers. Because I was basically on my own (and so was she), we hung together real hard. She showed me how to get into the nightclubs downtown, places to go when we ditched school, and how to take care of myself with no money. My father had long since given up on trying to control my every move. He told me that my mother sent me there because I wanted to be grown, he gave me an ultimatum. I could follow his rules and receive whatever I needed to survive and be happy or I could do whatever I wanted and meet my own needs for survival. I chose to be on my own while I was out there. I didn't have to answer to him, tell him where I was going, or when I'd be back. In addition, I could not ask him for anything or come to him with my troubles. I'd have to figure life out on my own, just as the adults did. I'm sure he was trying to teach me a lesson on the need to get guidance from my parents, but he had underestimated how much like him and my mom I really was. Having to figure life out on my own was right up my alley. That's all I wanted anyway, to be on my own, to answer to no one but myself (or so it seemed). Rhonda didn't have to really answer to anyone either. Her Aunt was raising her and her three younger sisters. One of her brothers lived with her dad and her older brother was in college. Because their mom had died with them so young they all had a certain sense of freedom. No one wanted to put too much pressure on them because they had lost her. Summer was coming, the weather was getting warmer, and the school year was coming to an end. I was being a free spirit, seeing who I wanted to see and doing what I wanted to do. I came and left whenever I wanted and worked odd jobs for my money. My dad had presented me with the ultimatum and I was meeting the challenge. I knew I would probably not pass any of my classes because I wasn't really going to school. I would show up to find Rhonda, find out what would be going on after school and to get out of the snow. I had very little interest in attending class. I had reasoned that I'd go back to LA and pursue an acting career and that I had no need for any other information they were trying to shove down my throat in school. Besides, it was really no big deal, I would just take the classes again the next year.

My first real job was as an Andy Frane usher. Rhonda and I went down together. They hired us both. It was my responsibility to escort theater goers to their seats at the various convention centers and concert halls. I loved working for them because I got to see all the concerts, plays, and dance performances for free. I got to see the Earth, Wind, & Fire concert, the Alvin Ailey Dancers, and The Jeoffrey Ballet, just to name a few. It was the coolest experience I had, so far, as an *"adult"*. One weekend I remembered being really tired. I had been out parting and had stayed out too late. I was supposed to work that Saturday and Sunday. I decided to sleep in for the weekend and call the company on Monday. When I called on Monday, they told me all I needed to do was turn in my uniform and pick up my last check. I was crushed. I couldn't comprehend why they didn't understand that I was too sick to call. There was no way for me to get word to them that I would not be working. With my mother being in a coma and my father working three jobs, I was the only one there to take care of my four little brothers and I was deathly ill. "Don't you get it", I said; "Don't you care". My family needed my income, I couldn't lose my job. It was my money that bought the family food. Even though it was a good story (or so I thought), they knew I was lying. I was actually shocked they didn't believe me. This was the first lesson in what it meant to THINK that I didn't have to answer to anyone, and I missed it. I would have to take this class again.

The rest of the summer went by without much incident. I didn't go to California to visit my mother but that was OK, we talked often. I hung out with Rhonda, went to the skating rink, played in the street, and watched the parade of women going in and out of Theodore's house. My father and I didn't talk much during this time and I didn't care. I felt he was just angry that he wasn't in control of my life anymore and that he would get over it eventually. Halimah continued to talk to me about different life incidents and give me advice when I asked. It was cool talking to her because she didn't treat me like a child. She was the liaison and mediator for me and my dad.

It was the fall of 1977, time to go back to school. I was failing Physical Science, for the second time, and there was this boy who had been following me around school. No one really knew that I failed out the previous year and that I wasn't a senior. I had a senior ID, I hung out in the senior lounge, and all my friends were seniors. But this boy was a junior, just like me. He wasn't cute at all. He was dark in complexion, about my height, and he wore glasses. His glasses had a nice frame but the lenses were really thick and he was goofy looking. Every time he saw me, he would break into this really big, goofy grin. One day I was walking down the hall and he was following me. I stopped and said "why do you keep following me". He said, "My name is Terrance and I'm in love with you." I broke into the hardest laugh I can remember. I told him there was no way I was going to date him and if he didn't stop following me, I would tell security he was harassing me. He said, "I

60

can't help it. I'm willing to face any consequence I have to just to get you to talk to me." When I got to my Physical Science class he followed me right inside. I knew then that he was crazy. My teacher said, "Why Terrance what are you doing here." I thought great, he was friends with the one teacher I couldn't stand. Terrance stood at the front of the class, in front of everyone and said, "That girl is going to be my woman and I'm going to follow her around everywhere she goes until she gives in." The teacher told him and everyone else, "I don't know why you want to be with her, she is failing this class. She is not intelligent enough to be of your caliber. You can do much better." I couldn't believe they were standing there talking about me as if I, and the rest of the class, weren't even there. Terrance told my teacher he didn't care if I was failing. He said he wanted me to agree to go out with him and he would be glad to help me with the class because he had already aced it the year before. The teacher was laughing, the class was laughing, he had that goofy grin, and even I managed a little chuckle, but no one said a word. Terrance finally said, "well?" I said, "what?" he said, "will you go out with me?" I said, "no way!" the rest of the class was chanting "GO, GO, GO". He said, "I'm not leaving until you say yes". My teacher said, "Ms. Bahar, you are disrupting my class and need to agree so we can get on with today's lesson." Reluctantly, I agreed, but only after he promised he would leave the class. So me and The Professor started what would become the best friendship I would experience in all of my stay in Chicago. He looked like a square but there was nothing square about him. We did everything together. We ditched school together. He taught me to play chess and scrabble, introduced me to new jazz artist, and pencil long reefer joints. Terrance made me laugh and for that I made him my best friend. The first time Terrance was to come to my house I warned him about Theodore, who would still harass guys occasionally just for kicks. Terrance assured me that he wasn't worried about Theodore because no one had been able to outrun him yet. I adored his honesty and gave him my address. After his first visit with me, I walked Terrance out to the end of the driveway. I was going to walk him to the corner to make sure that Theodore didn't bother him but he didn't want me to. He told me that Theodore would just have to get used to him coming around because it had taken a lot to get me to go out with him and he certainly wasn't going to lose me by backing down from some neighborhood bully. That, I liked, I liked it a lot. Theodore was the first to stand up to my dad and Terrance was the first to stand up not only to my dad but also to Theodore. That in itself was worthy of my attention, and Terrance became my best friend.

I had been introduced to marijuana when I was at Henry Clay. Stephanie, my cousin Teresa, and I would skip school to drink and get high. When I came to Chicago the first time I continued that practice. It wasn't ironic that now living in Chicago, my two new best friends, Terrance and Rhonda, and I would turn this practice into a daily habit. Even though Terrance looked square, he really was living a double life. At school he took on the persona of The Professor, at home he was cool. He was raised by his Aunt Joan and Uncle Tommy. His mother had died of an overdose when he was young. His father had run off long before that and his stepfather was a drug dealer. He had a little brother Cedrick, who was being raised by another aunt at the time. Joan and Tommy were really cool because they kept big grocery bags of weed all the time. They didn't mind me being over there and they didn't mind us smoking. There were many days when me and Terrance would sit around his house smoking weed, drinking, and listening to jazz. I had never met a teenager that liked jazz as much as I did. I had the strong misconception that I was living life as an adult. Terrance and I had a lot in common. We thought alike in a lot of things but he was much smarter than me. He could roll numbers around in his head in any form then bring them together to a solution without even writing anything down. He was also a gentleman. There were nights when I had stayed too late, he would catch the bus with me all the way home then get back on the bus to return home.

Something was different in me. I wasn't the young girl who arrived in Chicago. Working at my first job, having my heart broken by my first love Theodore and being well into building a solid relationship with Terrance, somehow I felt really grown even though I was only 16.

Looking back, and knowing what I know now, 16 should be an age of extended innocence. It should be a time to explore moderate independence. But I'd already experienced so much that I felt old. I felt like somehow life was passing me by too quickly. I didn't know then just how minor my experiences were. It never resonated just how young I was and that I had a lot more living to do.

I had not seen my mother and she wanted me to come home for Christmas. I wanted to stay in Chicago to watch how they did Christmas in the snow, but I knew I would have a better Christmas at home. My father didn't celebrate Christmas and there would be no real festivities around our house so I went home. When I got to LA I was hit with a burst of excitement. It was hot, everybody had the shopping bug, my house was decorated, and my little brother Jack had gotten so big that I hardly recognized him. When I left he was this annoying little boy who was always getting on my nerves. When I got back, he was tall, he had a little curly natural, and he was talking none stop. All of my family and friends were glad to have me back for the holidays. My cousin Teresa had a son, Johnny Jr. and Stephanie was pregnant, about to be married. My stepfather, David, was asking me all these questions about Chicago and my dad. I had given David the blues every chance I got since he married my mother when I was seven. I didn't like him and wasn't even sure why. I treated him very badly all during my childhood even tried to accuse him of attempted rape. It was amazing how he never turned his back on me even after everything I had done to him. My grandmother, Piggy, wanted to make sure that my father wasn't poisoning my mind and spirit with all that Muslim stuff. There had been a battle for my soul between daddy and piggy for many years. Piggy was a Christian minister and she wanted to ensure my salvation by loading me down with as much of the Bible as she could within anytime she had with me. Daddy was a Muslim minister and he wanted to make sure I knew how to be cautious of the white man and all of his devilish deeds. He didn't want me vulnerable to the white man's ability to physically, mentally, and spiritually rape the black woman. Overall I had a good time during my Christmas vacation. When I first arrived my mother found condoms in my suitcase. Deducing that I was sexually active, she sat me down with some of her birth control pills and THE talk. She explained that they were hers and may be a bit strong for me. Since I was only home for a couple of weeks she didn't have time to get me checked so I could have my own. I would do that when I returned in the summer. Until then I was to take hers as she prescribed and if I had any trouble with them I was to stop taking them immediately.

Christmas vacation was coming to an end and it was time for me to return to Chicago. I was sad about leaving but looking forward to returning to Terrance. When I landed at the airport it was freezing. It was so hot in LA that I forgot to bring extra clothes for the trip home from the airport in Chicago, but I survived. Not long after I returned, I began to break out into rashes but only at night never in the daytime. I thought it was those pills my mother had given me so I stopped taking them. I talked to Halimah about the possibility of getting pregnant. She told me about being a young girl and always wanting a daughter. She had gotten pregnant when she was very young and didn't think she was ready for the responsibility. She opted not to have the child then preceded to give birth to four boys in a row. She believed that the first child she didn't have was the daughter she always wanted and that now she would not be given the opportunity to have that daughter. She believed this was the price she had to pay for taking that life, however necessary it was at the time. Her story impacted me in a deep and powerful way. It set in place a belief system that would later dictate how I would decide to deal with ANY child that God would bless me to carry. From her story, I came to believe that having a life seed planted in my body was a gift from God. How I cared for that seed would be my gift back to God. She told me the best way to deal with pregnancy was to take necessary precautions to avoiding a pregnancy I was not ready to carry to full term. I thanked her for her advice and held onto the information until it was needed.

Returning to school was no big deal. Just like the year before, I wasn't attending many classes. I continued to put off my responsibilities throughout the rest of the semester. The impact of my actions didn't hit me until the end of the school year came. It was an ordinary day on the bus headed to my school. I got on at my usual stop, greeted all my friends at their perspective stops. We chattered on and on along the way. When we approached the stop at Kenwood, I gathered my things to exit the bus. Everyone was looking at me puzzled. When I asked why everyone was staring at me, Rhonda asked me why I was getting off the bus. I said I was going to school and asked where everyone else was going. Rhonda said they were going to the Aerie Crown Theater for graduation practice and asked wasn't I graduating. My heart dropped. These were the people I had been hanging out with in the senior lounge all year. These were the people that I had been skipping classes with all year. These were the people that had taught me how to play the card games, bid whiz, straight whiz, tunc, and board games, backgammon, ace deuce, and chess. These were the people I had smoked weed with on the "reefer row" wall. We had gone to the prom, the senior picnic, the lake, and ditch parties together. We had done it all. But on this day, I was getting off the bus and they were going on to graduate. Somewhere in there they had managed to attend their classes and get their studies done, I had not. I felt alone. I felt like the butt of some cruel joke. The lesson my father had been telling me I'd learn one day was becoming clear. I had been putting everything off for tomorrow and now tomorrow was here and I still had not put in the work. I stood there as the bus pulled off that day and watched in humiliation as all my friends went off to the next phase of their lives. I headed across the street to school to introduce myself to all the teachers I had dodged that year. In the next 4 weeks of school I put in a lot of work for my teachers. Some of them were disgusted that I was making such high marks on the work because they would still not be able to pass me on my absence alone. One teacher sat me down one day and told me that I was much too smart to give up on school. He told me that if I attended summer school and applied myself really hard, I could graduate the following year. He didn't know that I would not be there the following year. He didn't know that I'd be back in LA and neither did I. I promised him I would give all that I had and finish. I just knew that when I told my dad that I wasn't graduating but was willing to give 100% this time, he would let me stay. This way I could be a senior for real and spend my senior year with Terrance. We could graduate together and plan our future at the same pace. It was June of 1978 and I would be 18 in July. I rationed that by the time I graduated in 1979 I would be an adult legally and I could take whatever steps next that I chose. To my surprise, when I told my dad about my graduation he said that he already knew. He told me that my mom sent me to Chicago to finish school and that it was his fault that I didn't do that on time. My time there was finished and it was time for me to return home. Since I wasn't going to be 18 for two weeks, I had no say so on what would happen to me next. I couldn't believe I had spent all this time in Chicago and I didn't have anything to show for it. I was devastated. I just knew my dad would give me another chance to prove I could accomplish something great. But since he didn't, I had to suck up my disappointment and make the most of the time I had left.

The last few days in Chicago, I spent with Rhonda and Terrance. Terrance said the same thing that Theodore had said. He would finish his last year in high school and he would move to LA to attend college. I would go back to high school in LA and finish. I had been here before so I was certain that this time I would not mess up. This time I would stick to the plan. One night I was at Rhonda's aunt's house. Terrance came over and we were playing with the Ouija board. Terrance didn't want to play because he said it was evil. Terrance had always talked about having a family once we were finished with all this school stuff. I asked the board would I have Terrance' baby one day. I was surprised when the board said yes. I labeled the board a joke, we went on with the day. We playfully discussed how our life would be with our small family. We laughed and giggled as we talked about where we would live, what kind of house we would have, how he would work and I would stay home with the kids. We would enjoy our own little picture perfect happily ever after. We soon said our good-byes and went on about our lives.

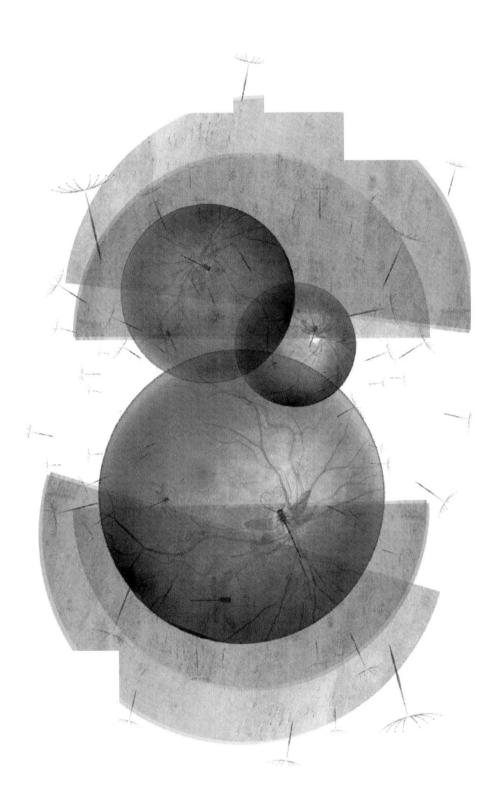

"Has this world been so kind to you that you should live with regret? There are better things ahead then anything we leave behind"
C.S. Lewis

Chapter 4

Home 4 Good

My dad not giving me any other options, I returned to Chicago. My cousin Teresa had set up a home for LA mid June 1978. A lot had happened while I was in herself and her family. I started hanging out with her a lot because she and John Sr. had their own apartment and a car. I'd go over there and kick it with her and Johnny Jr. all day. One day she lit a cigarette and it made me so nauseous that I had to throw up. She asked me how long that had been happening and I told her not that long. Teresa said, "Girl you are pregnant." I laughed it off and told her she didn't know what she was talking about. She took me to this free clinic that confirmed it to be true. The thoughts in my head began to swirl. My mother would be devastated, my father would hate me, and Terrance. What would Terrance do? After all, he was really only a child. I was a child too but because of my new condition, I put myself in the position of being forced to grow up immediately. He had no way of coming here to LA now. What about his future, he was smart, he had a future. I couldn't ask him to drop everything and accept this unexpected responsibility. What about what Halimah said. I wanted a daughter one day too. I didn't want to be punished for the rest of my life for taking this life. I didn't know what to do. Teresa sat down and talked to me for a long time. Think about this Zina, she said. It is a big responsibility, it's not easy. There is a lot more to it than what you see. I did think about it, I knew what was involved in taking care of a kid. I had been involved in bringing up all my siblings. That was a big responsibility and that wasn't even the half of it. What about school? I wanted to keep the promise I made to finish. How would I take care? I talked to Stephanie, she was married now and her baby was born. She told me to think twice because even though they were both there, it was still very hard. They had very little time to themselves, it was very expensive, and a crying baby is no joke. I sat with my stomach one night. I talked to God and I talked to my baby. I asked them what they wanted me to do. I reminded them both that if I went through with this it would probably be just me and them. I told them that my father would probably disown me and Terrance could very well disappear and never return. I told them that if this was the course that I was to take that I needed to know from them that we could make it even if no one else stayed in our life. Were they willing to stay when everybody else left? The answer was yes, and I made the decision to have it. Now I was faced with the task of letting everyone else know about my decision. Terrified, I finally managed to tell my mother and she said she already knew, she was just waiting for me to say something. She wanted me to take everything in consideration and see that the best thing was to not have it. I told her that wasn't going to be my decision and although she wanted to be supportive, she was not going to make this easy for me. If this was going to be my decision then I needed to be ready to take it on in full and be prepared to not ask for her help in any way. I agreed, remembering my conversations with God and my baby. When I told Terrance, he said he was not prepared for this and wished I would reconsider what I should do. Realizing my mind was made up, he would make some adjustments to his plans to accommodate his part of the responsibility. I let him know that I understood that this was completely unexpected and that if he chose not to be a part of this child's life, I would assume full responsibility of its care, and tell the child that its father had died before it was born. He was determined to try and help as much as he could. Instead of going to college he would join the army and add the child on as a dependent so money could be sent on its behalf. He let me know that it would extend the length of time we had to be apart. He stated that we should be realistic about our ability to have a relationship and that we should consider going on with our lives individually. He promised that he would not leave me hanging with the child alone no matter what my decision about us was going to be. My father's reaction to the news brought up a lot of the feelings I had when I told Theodore about Antonio Giovanni. He was bitter and angry, he asked me how I could do this to him. He reminded me of the time he gave me my ultimatum. When I chose my freedom, the only thing he asked is that I take care not to get pregnant while I was under his care. I had failed at the only thing he had asked of me. It cut very deep that I had let him down so, but my decision was made. It was time for me to move on now. My mother thought it best for me to get a job before I began to show. She pulled some strings for me at TRW. I was hired and trained as an assembler. I hated it but I wanted to be responsible and make sure I could provide a life for me and my child. I applied for medical, food stamps, and WIC so I could get medical attention and buy my own food. With every check, I would go to KMART and buy something I thought my baby would need. I was stocking up on pampers, tee-shirts, rattles and toiletries. I had gotten a bed from somewhere and was putting other household items on layaway to be ready once I got an apartment. I was determined to show my mother that I could handle this responsibility without her assistance. I didn't want my child to be born to a mother who wasn't even a high school graduate so I began attending night school. Naturally I returned to Washington because I knew the staff there. My counselor suggested I go for my GED and I did. When the results returned my counselor expressed his disappointment. He said that my scores were amongst the top ten in the country and with scores like that I could been a straight "A" student with college scholarship potential. It was him that encouraged me to attend night school. He said that a GED was as good as a high school diploma in CA, but that it held no bearing in any other state. He told me that if I added 4 night school classes with my GED scores I could get my actual diploma and it would be good in any state I went to. Since I was secretly planning to return to Chicago to raise my child, I thought it'd be a good idea to be a high school graduate. Terrance came down for the Christmas holiday to visit with me and meet my mother and her side of the family. Even though my mom was still very angry with me, and getting angrier as I got bigger, she was as pleasant as she could be while Terrance was here. He talked endlessly about having a plan to make sure that I was not alone in taking care of the baby. But mom was not convinced. When he left, she told me I would never see him again and that I better be prepared to do this by myself. She didn't know about my long talks with God and my baby. She didn't know that I made that decision before even telling anyone that I was pregnant. She didn't know that me and my baby would take this world by surprise even if everybody left. What I didn't know is that everything she was trying to prepare me for was all the stuff she was not prepared for when she found herself alone with a child at the age of 20. My mother loved me beyond description and could only give me everything she had with what she knew at the time. It would be many years before I could understand and appreciate that. Up to now, and many years beyond here, what I thought about her and the things she did added up to her standing between me and anything I wanted with all of her selfish will. Another class I would have to repeat over and over before the lesson was learned. In January TRW had a big layoff. I found myself 7 months pregnant and out of work. I knew that unemployment would not be enough to care for my child so I applied for public assistance. I was not raised on the county so I thought it would not be long before I returned to the work place. Being in line all day at the county building, standing in line at the unemployment office, filling out all the paperwork as to why my baby's father was not in my life proved to be very stressful. One day in a fit of anger and frustration I had a classic tantrum. The first of a few breakdowns I would have over the next 20 years. The next day I went into labor. Even though my mother had not had very much to say to me over the previous weeks, on this day she showed up in full riot gear to be in support of her baby having a baby. I was awakened that morning when with a loud pop I realized my water bag had broken. I ran to the bathroom screaming "MAMMA, MAMMA". Sitting on the toilet with water running out of me, I said my water is breaking. My mom asked me how I knew, I said I didn't think I would be peeing for this length of time. When the water slowed down, we padded me as well as possible to make it to the hospital without being too wet. When we got there, they put me in a labor room. They began prepping me for delivery. I wasn't in any pain but I was a little nervous about what would take place next. My mother was in a chair next to my bed and we were talking. We talked more that morning than we had talked for years. Since I was already pregnant when I got home from Chicago, she was too angry to catch up on what my life had been like while I was out there. We talked about my dreams, what I thought my life would be like having to raise a child. I told her about my talks with God and my baby. She told me about all things she thought when she was caring me. She told me about the difficulties she had when she realized she would be raising me alone. She talked about how everything had changed in her life once she was alone. All the sacrifices she had to make. How she had to go from having goals and dreams to making sure she had an income that would support her and her daughter. I took it all in. It was good for us to bond at this time. We hadn't really talked like this for my whole pregnancy. I was happy to have my mom back. I listened to her and she listened to me. We laughed and when the pains began we cried. She told me that she really didn't expect me to handle this whole thing as well as I had and that she was really proud of me taking responsibility for my actions in spite of everything. I told her that I knew she believed Terrance and I were too young to do this, especially from such a great distance. I told her that we were going to try this and do the best we could to be good parents to our baby. She told me it was a nice dream and that she wished it would turn out like that but reality had a way of making dreams and wishes seem like childlike fantasies. That I shouldn't be too disappointed if it didn't turn out that way. I responded to that with the worst pain I had ever felt in my life. I screamed bloody murder and my mom ran to get the nurse. While she was gone they came to check me and determined that I was ready to deliver. When they got me into the delivery room, I only needed to push three excruciatingly painful times and my child was here. They cleaned my baby, sucked mucus from its nose, then proudly announced that it was a healthy baby boy. I had a son and he was precious. Cleaning him just a little, they wrapped him, and put him in a small, clear, bassinet. As they were wheeling us out to recovery, my mom came running down the hall. She was frantic, she said, "good you have her, what delivery room are you taking her to?" I said, "Mom, I had him, it's a boy." She asked, where is he? I pointed behind my head. From that very moment she was in love with him. All the anger she had with me during my pregnancy seemed to evaporate, it was as if it had never existed. I was too exhausted to care. I don't remember much about that moment except that he was headed to the nursery and I was headed to recovery to rest. Hallelujah!

Later that night, the nurse woke me up to receive my baby. I asked couldn't I get just a little more sleep. She simply replied, "Sure, once your baby is sleep." She told me this is your baby, you'll have to take care of him now. Your time to rest is over until he moves out in about 18-20 years from now. My mother came just as she was giving him to me. He was beautiful. He was creamy colored, he had fine, smooth, jet black, straight hair. His eyes were slanted and for a while he looked like a little Asian baby. Initially, I questioned him even being mine, but they reassured me that there were safeguards in place to ensure each child being given to the appropriate parent. My mom was holding him, when she asked me the question, "What are you going to name him?" Well, I thought I'd name him, Terrance the 2nd. She reminded me that Terrance would never be a part of his life and told me if I named him that she would never speak to me or him. I knew she didn't know any of Terrance' family so I said how about "Cedrick". She said OK, Cedrick is a nice name. Cedrick Anthony Mitchell, I said. "Mitchell?" she replied. Yes, I said, my dad doesn't go by Moorhead, and I hate that name, I'm certainly not going to make my son go by that name for the rest of his life. Reluctantly, she agreed, Cedrick Anthony it is.

There was a recall from the layoff at TRW shortly after Cedrick was born. I had gone through so much grief with the county and TRW was known to have frequent layoffs, so I decided not to reveal that I had returned to work. It's a good thing I didn't because I was only there for a few months before I was laid off again. This time they gave us the option of going over to XEROX if we could wait for 30 days, I gladly accepted. Since I was going to be off for the next month I decided to take

Cedrick to Chicago to meet my father and his. We were only there for a week and Terrance was clearly overwhelmed by the responsibility of taking care of a child. We knew for sure then that this would not work, but he would still go to the Army so I could at least get some child support. When I returned I worked and collected public assistance for the next year. I had my job, I was raising my son, I was being independent (not asking for help from any of my family). I was 18 years old and I was handling the cards life dealt to me pretty well. You really couldn't tell me anything.

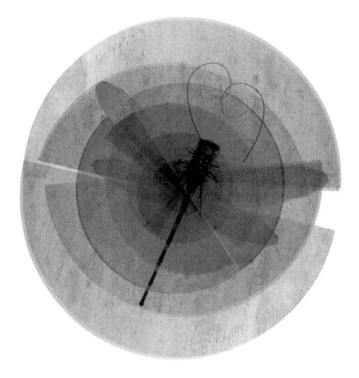

"My people are destroyed for lack of knowledge; because you have rejected knowledge, I also, reject you as my priests"
Hosea 4:6

CHAPTER 5

My Way or No Way

I was living life on my own terms, I didn't have to answer to anyone. I was partying with Teresa in LA, with Stephanie in Compton, with friends from work in Inglewood, and I was still living with my mom. My mother had this thing about "her rules". I needed to be in by a certain time and take care of my son a particular way. I didn't really get it but I wasn't going to try either. One day after a big argument about me being grown, with a child, she told me to "pack my stuff, get my baby, and get out". I went to work that day asked a good friend of mine if I could rent her camper home in the back of her house, she said I could. I took off of work, went home, packed my suitcase, picked up my layaway at KMART, and went to prepare my new home for me and my son. When my mom got off work, I called her to let her know that I had moved and that me and Cedrick were fine. Through tears she told me I didn't have to move that day. She told me she wanted me to move but not with anyone else, but if that was my decision then so be it. I told her I couldn't take her telling me to move out every week anymore. I told her it was time for me and Cedrick be on our own. I knew she didn't want me and Cedrick to live in a camper but it would only be until I found a place I could afford. The first time I had gotten fed up with her I moved in with this married man. He had an argument with his wife, she packed her stuff, grabbed their daughter and went to her mother's. I don't know why I thought that meant it was over, talk about naive. I moved in, gonna show my mother that I knew how take care of a family. Two weeks later I had to have my mother come move me and Cedrick back because Tanya wanted to come home to her husband. This was one lesson I got right off the bat and I couldn't wait for the day when he would return and I would be able to say, "I'M

SORRY, BUT YOU MISSED YOUR CHANCE!". That day did come about six months later and I relished in the opportunity. But this time I had the money to move, I just needed to find a place for the right price that I liked. A couple of months later I found my very first apartment on 108th and Vermont. It was a one bedroom apartment for $150 a month. I was making $10 per hour at XEROX, $600 per month with public assistance, and $60 per month in food stamps. My car was paid for, my utilities were cheap, my rent was cheap, and I was buying a $10 bag of weed and Tangueray Gin & lime juice every week on pay day. I made up the rules of my life as I went along. Me and Cedrick were always sharp, all my bills were paid, and I thought I had it made. The only thing I was missing was a steady boyfriend. I wanted to meet a guy who wanted to marry and have children. I always wanted a large family because basically I was an only child and I was very lonely. I wanted two sets of triplets, 3 boys then 3 girls, and I wanted them close in age. I didn't really want them all right then but that would be necessary if they were to be close in age because Cedrick was already here. Had I been paying attention to my lessons along the way, I would have known that I was set and needed only to secure my future from where I was standing and all the things I wanted would have come my way. But no, things couldn't be done like that, that would be much too simple.

It was the end of 1979, I was 19 years old and since I was raising my son by myself I thought I was full blown grown. I thought I had it going on and that I was succeeding at taking care of myself. Somewhere in here, my priorities got all screwed up. It was at this time in my life that I lost all sight of where I wanted my life to go. It was right here that reality came in and turned all my dreams and goals into childlike fantasies. I no longer pursued my dreams of being a dancer. I no longer wanted a career as an actress. I didn't even think of modeling. I didn't care about the plan that Terrance and I had created. My life revolved around smoking weed, drinking Tanqueray Gin & lime juice, hanging up at Teresa's or at Stephanie's, and looking for a father for my son. I thought I needed a husband for me and a father for Cedrick (and the rest of the children I thought I was supposed to have right away) so he would not feel the loneliness of being an only child. Right here I got lost. I felt like something was missing. Ever since the rape I had been running from one man to another. Every relationship that I thought would last a life time failed. Every accomplishment that made me feel strong was matched by a sense of low self-worth. I didn't see myself as a viable candidate for a wife. It was right here, in my season of being lost, that he found me. Rondell was a tall skinny guy that lived across the street from me. His family actually lived in the house that my uncle Scotty, Teresa's father, lived in when we were at Henry Clay. He lived with his grandmother Loretta, his mother Doris, and his 6 sisters Tasha, Jenny, Janice, Annette, Jackie, and Tamia. He also had a brother, Oliver, who lived with his father. Janice and Tamia use to sit with Cedrick when I went out. Tasha moved to Compton with her three children. Jenny moved next door to me with her daughter. He followed me around for weeks until I agreed to go out with him. Looking back, I see that every relationship I've been in started because someone would not leave me alone. The men pursued me the same way that my rapist did. He followed me from block to block until he cornered me and I had no place to turn. I knew I couldn't run & get away. I knew I couldn't fight & win. I didn't even try to resist, I just surrendered. Because of my low self-esteem I responded in the same way in my relationships, I just surrendered when I felt cornered! Today they call that stalking and it's illegal. The same thing happened with Rondell. I didn't try to make sure he was a viable candidate for a husband or father. He followed me around until one day I did go out with him and before long he was living with me. Terrance was in the Army sending Cedrick allotment checks of $150 each month. He had gone on with his life and there was no angst between us. Rondell asked me to marry him and on July 11, 1979 we were married. Just 2 weeks later on July 16, we got the phone bill and Rondell was so angry about me being in touch with Terrance that he said "if we weren't married he would have left me". Rondell had a jealous streak that I didn't see before. I had to stop talking to all my friends that he didn't know. I had to report my every move. My life had been reduced to the routine going to work and back home without me even noticing it. If I knew what I was in for, I would have let him go right then. But I stayed

for the sake of my son. The next time Terrance called for me, Rondell

got the call and told him that "he was Cedrick's father now and not only

did we not need his money but he didn't want him calling anymore".

Terrance being a child himself and only having seen Cedrick once

agreed without argument. Just as my mother had predicted, we never

saw Terrance again. I continued to keep in touch with Terrance' aunt and

uncle secretly. I called twice a year every year but they were so angry

that I ruined his chance to attend college that they were usually guarded

in telling me where he was at any given time. I know at the beginning he

was somewhere in Atlanta but he changed his station a number of times.

Eventually we lost contact and my only connection was his aunt and

uncle who were not very receptive of me and my child. My marriage to

Rondell was like two children playing house, with neither one of us

having a home to go to when the game was over. Our intentions were

genuine but we were much too ill-equipped to make a marriage work at

this time.   Because there was no emotional maturity to accept our separate responsibilities, there was a lot of time spent blaming one another for the things that were not right between us. But we did not know that so we kept trying because I believed that once you get married, you STAY married. I also believed that Rondell loved Cedrick and I didn't want to take that away. Rondell was so taken with Cedrick that he really wanted a child of his own. Although I wanted more children, I knew it was not a good time to have one. My understanding of what a wife was to do for her husband was distorted and I thought it was my duty to submit. I believed that a wife should accommodate herhusband at every opportunity. I didn't think it was my place to deny him a child of his own. On October 15, 1981 I gave birth to our son, DaWayne Alan. Initially Rondell was very excited to have a child on the way but halfway through the journey of my pregnancy, he changed. He became irritated by my constant cravings, mood swings, and demands on his time. By the time I was 9 months, he didn't even want a baby. He began to sleep around and all I wanted to do was drop this load so I could sleep around too, that would teach him. On October 14th, I caught

95

Rondell on the phone with another woman. I remembered that having a tantrum brought on labor with Cedrick so I picked a physical fight with Rondell to try and bring my labor down. It took a lot of bashing and abusing to get him to hit me back but finally after a stern slap in the face he swung and the fight was on. When we finished and my kitchen was trashed, I simply went to pack my overnight bag for the hospital. I placed my coat on the bed next to me and sat at the end of the bed to wait. At about midnight the first pain hit, I punched Rondell and said, get up, our baby is on its way. I didn't waste any time playing "mommie & me" games. Rondell had spent my whole pregnancy playing around while I stayed home fat and depressed. It was time for me to take my life back. The resiliency of women has always been amazing to me. I felt like I had been through the wringer. I felt like a middle age woman going through a middle age crisis. It's crazy that I was only 21 years old and I believed that my life was out control and going hay-wire. Now that my baby was here, it was time for me to get back to working, I knew I didn't want to go back to assembly work. Two months after I gave birth,

I enrolled in school. I took a 6 week PBX operator course at Trade Tech College. I got my certificate of completion in Feb of 82 and Mar 82 I got a job as a PBX operator at the Bonaventure Hotel. Me and Rondell moved to a larger apartment on the Eastside and my cousin Rose, her husband J.T., and their 2 children moved with us. I worked the 3pm to 11pm shift and when I got home Rose would be up waiting for me. We would smoke weed, drink wine, eat monkey bread with cheese, and play cards throughout the night. Again, I was making my own rules as I went, I was being an adult. It is amazing that I was only 22 years old and so much had happened in my life already. Rose and J.T. moved their family to Long Beach. J.T. found Rondell a job out there and began the task of moving my family to a new city. Other than Chicago, I had never really relocated on my own but I was ready for the task. I found a nice two bedroom apartment in Long Beach for our family, my husband was working in Long Beach, and we were being responsible. I had forgiven his many infidelities and he had forgiven my one, or so we thought. At some point in here we begin to have disagreements that were not being resolved. We would get mad, have these knockdown, drag out fights, stop speaking, get horny, have sex, and never go back to the issue that created the argument in the first place. During one of these make up sex sessions, we did not have any protection. I wanted to have sex but I wanted him to go to the store for protection first. He said the mood would change if he left and that if we were careful, we should be all right. I reminded him about my issue with abortions and that if a pregnancy did occur, we'd have to deal with it because I would definitely keep the baby. He knew that I believed the gift of life to be a tremendous honor and blessing. I would never end the possibility of life with an abortion. In the heat of this moment he said fine. Six pregnant months later, at a pre-natal appointment, we found out I was having twins. It was Mar 1983 and he had already told me if I kept the baby that our marriage would not survive the pregnancy. Now, at 6 months pregnant, I find out I'm having twins. I didn't care, I'd rather have to deal with the wrath of Rondell than the wrath of God. Sure enough, in April he left. We had moved to a 3 bedroom condo in Long Beach. It was a difficult time because I was 23 years old, I had 2 toddler sons, I was pregnant with twins, I was still on the county, and I was alone. I couldn't really do much because I kept threatening to miscarry. I spent a lot of that time crying and sitting around being pitiful. During one episode of false labor, my mother came, packed up my little family, and moved us to her house. I hated having to be rescued by my mother. I was angry and ashamed that my husband had left me. Again, it looked like she was right about me not knowing how to make adult decisions. One more time my decisions landed me in a position where I was unable to take care of myself or my family. Again, I needed her help. She was living next door to my grandmother on 95th and Vermont at the time. She had a 2 bedroom house with a patio converted into a bonus room. The rooms were small so she designated the entire den to me and my growing family. 95th street was like an incubator for my family. It was a nice tree lined neighborhood in South Central Los Angeles. There were mostly Caucasian families when she moved there but it had transitioned to more African Americans during my lifetime. My grandmother had bought the house on 95th and Vermont before I was born, in the early 60's. She was one of the first African Americans to own a home on that block. My mother left my father when I was two and my grandmother, along with her 3rd husband, bought the house next door, and let me and my mom have the house she was in. When my grandmother left her husband, she moved back into the house next door. My mother bought the house next to that and my great grandmother moved here from Arkansas into the house across the street. So here I am on the county, in a failing marriage, with my 2 sons, pregnant with my 3rd & 4th children, 23 years old, and I have to live with my mother on a block with 3 generations of matriarchal family control. I hated it, I felt like a complete failure. Living my life by the rules I had made was not working. Everything my mother had said was coming true. But I still did not let go of the idea that she did not really know what was best for me. I still did not get that everybody has to answer to somebody. I was still fighting for the right to not have to answer to anybody. I was still not learning my lessons. On May 26, 1983, I gave birth to two beautiful, identical, twin girls. Shawna Letrece and Keyanna Caprice. My own little Brady bunch was coming together. If I could only get this husband to act right, we'd be the perfect little family. When they were 1 week old I went back to my own home, in Long Beach CA, to raise my family. I was determined not to let my mother be the victor, my family was going to survive my poor ability to make decisions. I tried desperately to get Rondell to come home, but he wouldn't. There was a lot of things about me he wanted to change, but I was certain it was him that needed the change. I was right and if he would just see that, we could both be happy. When the twins were 6 weeks old, the Bonaventure told me if I didn't return to work in a week, I would lose my job. My sister in law, Tasha, would come to my house and baby sit while I worked.

"I form the light and create darkness, I make peace and create calamity. I, the Lord, do ALL these things"
Isaiah 45:8

CHAPTER 6

Cocaine

There was a girl at work that I rode home with. One night she needed to make a stop after work. We went to a friend of hers that had a really nice apartment. It was clearly a bachelor pad. There was black leather furniture with multi-colored pillows to one side and a black lacquered entertainment center to the other. In the dining room sat a smoked glass top dining table with high back black and grey, clothe chairs. In the kitchen was mahogany cabinets with brown, speckled granite counter tops. They were smoking cocaine rocks from this table mirror. It was a little strange that she trusted me to know this side of her but she knew I smoked weed so I guess she figured it would be ok. She showed me how to place the rock on the pipe, how to hold the torch under the bowl of the pipe and how to draw the smoke. I tried it but didn't really understand the high, there were too many rules to getting high this way. It made me sick to my stomach, I threw up and I was ready to go. She convinced me that I was just doing it wrong so every so often I would go with her after work and we'd get high for a while then go home. After a few months of that, I decided that this just wasn't the high for me, I had a family to look after, and so I stopped.

My grandmother hated that I had to work and not be with my children. She came from the old school where husbands went to work and wives stayed home to look after the kids until they reached a certain age. She asked me why I was leaving all my children during their developing years to work, where was my husband, why wasn't he taking care of us? Ashamed that I couldn't keep my husband home, I told her that it didn't matter where my husband was, all I knew is that he wasn't there. I said that I had to work because I couldn't continue to transport my children on the bus and that I needed to get us a car. She asked me if I had a car,

104

would I stop working and raise my children myself. I said yes and she bought me a little, yellow, stick shift, pinto. The condition was that I had to stop working and I couldn't let Rondell drive the car. Since Rondell had taken 2 other cars I had helped pay for, on 2 previous breakups, I agreed without hesitation. I got the car, quit my job, and went home to raise my four children by myself. Then I had an emotional shut down. I began to cry uncontrollably, I was unable to get out of bed and I didn't want to eat. I was tired all the time and I became very depressed about the condition of my life. I couldn't really put my finger on it, but from the outside it looked like Rondell was living the life of riley and I was bogged down with the responsibility of raising these kids and paying all my bills alone. He was living with his mother and dating other women and I was home trying to figure out how to raise my family and pay my bills on $900 dollars a month from the county. One day the twins were asleep on the pallet I made for them on the floor. Cedrick and DaWayne were playing close by. Cedrick hit DaWayne which made him cry softly. DaWayne hit Cedrick back, which made him scream. The scream startled both the twins and they woke up screaming. I stood back looking at the picture of all four of my children crying and I didn't know who to settle first. I couldn't take it anymore, my life was simply too hard for a person my age. It wasn't supposed to be this way. This wasn't how I imagined my life would be. I wanted to scream and in my frustration, I just sat down on the floor, screamed and cried with them. I knew then that we would not make it, and I really didn't even want to make it. I was simply tired. I thought about how I could kill all the children then commit suicide, and we'd all be gone. Yes, that was it; that was the only solution. So this was it, this was how it would all come to an end. Just then, the doorbell rang and interrupted my thoughts. It was Tasha, with her 3 children. With a big smile she said, "Hi honey, I'm home." I just cried and fell into her arms, she was a God send, and she was my angel. Without knowing it, she saved my life and lives of my children. Tasha had left her kid's father and with nowhere to go, she asked if she and the kids could move in with me. That God that I was losing faith in came through just in the nick of time. It was the summer of 1983, and we had it down to a science. Tasha shared her bedroom with her youngest daughter. I shared my bedroom with the twins, and our four boys had a room to themselves. Every morning we would get up and one of us would fix breakfast while the other one would get kids clothes ready for the day. The kids would eat and then we would start the assembly line. One would bath kids while the other dressed kids. Once the older ones were dressed and outdoors playing, we'd clean and dress the twins to ready them for their naps, because it would be near noon by now. Once they were laid out on their floor pallets, me and Tasha would start dinner, get a Champale, and smoke the first joint of the day. At some point the kids would come in for lunch. We would feed them their lunch, lay them down for naps and the twins would wake for afternoon feedings. When the older ones would wake from their naps, we'd get them situated for early evening TV, and walk to the corner store for our 4 pack champales. She would get pink and I would get golden. On the way back from the store we'd smoke our second joint of the day. When we returned from our evening walks, toasted and mellow, we would serve dinner and prepare for the night time assembly line. When dinner was done, one of us would do baths while the other would dress them for bed. By 8pm every night the kids would have had a full day of play and be in bed for the night. With jazz playing in the background, we'd share the duty of cleaning up from dinner. We'd lay out on the floor for a couple of hours of drinking the last two champales, from the previous days walk, and smoke the last joint of the day. Then we would giggle our way to sleep talking about all the antics we had seen in the condo complex during the day. The next day we would start the process over again. It was the coolest summer I'd had for a long time. We worked together as a team. We should have known it was too good to last. I guess Rondell didn't like that I was REALLY ok without him. Up to now, anytime he left, I would spend the whole time he was gone begging him to come back. He always felt secure in the fact that I would not be able to find a man that would want to be with me and all these kids. He didn't figure that I might get comfortable with my life without a man. He came to me one night close to the end of the summer, and asked if we could try again. I was hesitant because I really didn't want Tasha to leave. She was more help to me than Rondell had ever been and I wanted her to stay just a little longer. Her Ex had been begging her to come home to. I knew if she left and things didn't work with me and Rondell, she would not come back and I'd be alone again. But I succumbed, and we tried again.

We moved into a little 3 bedroom cottage around the corner on 22nd and Myrtle in Long Beach. We continued to fight and breakup. This only lasted for a few months and after one of those breakups, I moved to a small 3 bedroom house on 21st and Atlantic. I was able to handle the rent on my own. I was still on the county but I was beginning to get small job assignments with different temp agencies. Everything was OK, and I was determined not to continue this whole yo-yo thing with Rondell. I hadn't done that since I was with Theodore, and I certainly didn't intend on continuing it with Rondell just because he was my husband. No one knew about the "me" that had learned from my mother how to let people go and let them know they had missed their chance with me. It was time for me to get back to her. The "her" that I used to be. The "her" that learned from my mother not to give 2nd chances. The "her" that knew how to move forward from a relationship and not look back. Rondell didn't deserve anymore chances and I thought I was done with him forever. I didn't know how I had come to this place in my life anyway. This wasn't who I was. I didn't have time to retrace my steps and see where I had gotten off my path or what my original path really was. But I was clear that whatever it was I wanted, didn't include being with some child in a man's body trying to play grown up and control my life, when he didn't even have the right rule book. I tried to find alternative activities. I would only go around people who had kids because they seemed to have the same patience I did. I had basically left all my friends when I got with Rondell. I did keep in touch, occasionally with Teresa and Stephanie. Every so often I would call back to Chicago to check in with Rhonda, Terrance' aunt and uncle, and ask my brothers about how Theodore was doing. Rhonda was in Florida modeling for Essence. I saw her picture once in Jet, she was the center fold. Theodore was still holding a torch for me, but I wasn't ready to talk to him directly yet. I still fantasized about being with Theodore. I wondered how things would have been different if I had waited and married him. Terrance' aunt and uncle would take my messages but I believed that they never delivered them. I was certain that if he was getting my messages, that he would have contacted me. I still did not know where he was and didn't have any way to let him know where we were. Teresa had left John and his mother had custody of Johnny Jr. The rumor was that she was hooked on cocaine, but I didn't believe that. Stephanie had left her husband but was raising her two sons alone. It was with her that I was re-introduced to smoking cocaine again and this time I actually got the high. I didn't get it before but I understood now that it was a rush that took me really up high but only lasted for a short time. We did that every so often but her house would get kind of crazy with the people she would smoke with. They would gather around the table and stare at the plate with the dope. There was always an argument about who had more dope. She would have the most unlikely people over her house. They looked unclean, unshaven, they wore dirty clothes and for the most part they just looked outright homeless. I never wanted to smoke with the people she had over, they all seemed like such an unsavory crowd. Most of the time they were suspicious that someone had stolen some dope and they would end up in fights. I enjoyed my new found relationship with Cocaine but I couldn't help but think it would be better if I did it in a more serene environment. It was uncomfortable so I would just do it at home sometime. I would put on some smooth jazz or easy listening and chill while the kids would play outside. It was cool. It was so cool that I hardly noticed that I was beginning to get high more and more.

During this time I started to pay attention to the patterns with Rondell, because it seemed like I was ending up in the same place. I knew there had to be a pattern that I was missing, I just needed to watch. I noticed that Rondell would leave, I would beg him to come back, he would stay gone until I stopped asking him to return, then he would show up when I was getting use to him being gone. I would ask him to leave, but because he knew I had not had any sex, he would refuse and begin to undress. He knew I didn't want him to be with anyone else, so he would ask could I just do him a favor and have sex with him. I would submit and before I knew what had happened, we'd be living together again. The last time he came over and begin to undress, I told him if he continued he would be terribly embarrassed when I refused to undress with him. I didn't want him to be standing there naked while I was fully dressed telling him to get out. I knew if I were to remain strong, I'd have to get him to leave before he undressed. I had never tried this and didn't know if it would work or not. By the time he got to his belt buckle, I began to cry. I'm not sure why, but I was screaming for him not to take his clothes off. He knew if he kept undressing I would stop. When he began to unzip his pants I was screaming and crying uncontrollably. Realizing I was serious, he laughed in my face and told me to calm down. He said "he didn't really want to sleep with a base head anyway, he was just doing me a favor." He got dressed and as he was walking out he said, that he didn't want anyone else raising his kids but he wasn't worried about it because no one would want me with all these damn babies anyhow. He walked out laughing and calling me a drug addict. No-one had ever said that to me before, not even him. I figured he was just tripping because I didn't want him back. I knew I wasn't an addict. After all an addict was a person who didn't eat, bath, comb their hair, pay their bills or take care of their children. I was none of those things. I didn't have a problem with drugs. Weed was not a problem for me and I only did cocaine when I had the extra money. That wasn't that often and when I didn't have the money I didn't do it. To my knowledge, that was not the definition of an addict.

It was the end of 1983, I was 23 years old and this time, I was sure that my marriage to Rondell was over. I didn't care though because, I was back to living by my own rules. I didn't believe the things he said about me were true so I didn't care what he thought about me. I accepted being a single mother and started getting back to what I thought life was about, (getting high, taking care of my kids, and not answering to anybody.)

I would still visit with Rose and J.T. on a regular basis. But I felt a little uncomfortable because they seemed to be really involved with all the normal things a family would be involved in; homework, dinner, family games and discussions; I didn't want to be intrusive. They'd always say I was welcome, but I figured they were just being supportive. I had a girlfriend that I used to visit from the old townhouse named Sheena'. We had a lot in common. She was raising her three children alone. She was dating a guy named Michael who had a twin brother named Alvin. Michael was a musician and Alvin was a doctor. I became a regular hanger-on at Sheena's, with Mark and the band. We'd go to the studio, get high and listen to their music, determine which songs were best for the album, trip, argue, laugh, and kick it. Sheena's kids were a little older so they'd sit with my kids while we were at the studio and they'd all play together when I was at her house. Being around them so much, I had a lot of contact with Alvin and we started a non-committed relationship (friends with benefits). He was not so much the music buff, he was the more stable, sensible one. He was, however, interested in me. We began to date on a regular basis. Even though we weren't together, Rondell still complained about not wanting anyone around his kids. I realized this is what he said to keep anyone from being around me. Things were going nicely with Alvin. But after only a couple of months, I told him I was falling for him and he told me that he wanted a woman that didn't have any kids. I thought to myself, "Who did he think all these little people were in my house". He knew he would not deal my family, why would he use me this way. This was the 1st guy that I decided to trust to bring around my kids. I was devastated, Rondell's prediction about no-one wanting to me with all the kids was coming to life. If this is how Alvin felt, how many other guys would feel the same way? It hurt to think that Rondell might be right and that I would be alone for the rest of my life. But if Alvin's response to me having kids was the indicator, then it looked like this would be my new truth. I knew then that if I was going to have anything, I would have to work harder for it because there would never be a husband around to offer financial assistance. The time for sitting around getting high was over. I needed to get busy, I needed a job. I hadn't worked for a while, but I knew I could start with the temp agencies. Working at the Bonaventure gave me experience in data entry. That opened my options and increased my earning capacity. I registered with three agencies and they kept me working until J.T. got me a job with Continental Cable as a trouble shooter. My life was a lot like it was when I got that first apartment back in South Central with Cedrick, except I had four kids instead of one. I was in this three bedroom house on Atlantic and 26th, my little pinto was paid for, most of my bills were paid, and one more time I thought I had it made. I didn't need Alvin, Rondell, Terrance, or anyone else who thought they could just use me and go on with their lives. I continued to go around Sheena's in spite of Alvin. He certainly wasn't going to run me from my friend's house. After all, I was the actress, playing this role would be nothing. Life is just a great big stage play. In any situation I need only determine the set space, script lines, associate myself with the rest of the actors, know my character and play my part until curtain. Alvin would never know just how deeply it really hurt me to find out that my kids were the reason he didn't want to be with me. But none of that mattered now. Life was becoming a series of stage plays and I seldom knew which one I was in at any given time. My characters were becoming a blur. All the character roles I had been playing began to blend together. I didn't know who I was supposed to be at any given time. All the plot lines were becoming confused. I was losing my grip again. Every so often I would spend the weekend at Stephanie's and we'd smoke cocaine the whole time (I didn't know anything about addiction or recovery…YET). I began to walk in a daze, I wasn't working toward any goals. I didn't have any dreams. I was just going to work, coming home, feeding the kids, watching TV until I went to bed, and getting high on the weekends. I never had money anymore and didn't connect it to getting high so often. I was 23 and I felt old, very, very old. I didn't realize that depression had set in and it was getting worse. I got ready for work one day and when I went to my car my tire was flat. I didn't have a spare, didn't have the money to get it fixed or catch the bus, so I walked. Tardiness was already a problem but I figured getting there anyway that I could was better than not going at all. I rationed that my excuse was good and my diligence would be commended. When I got there I explained my situation and told my boss that I could not fix the tire until payday, which was the next day. I told him since it was Thursday I would probably be late again on Friday. He said nothing and I worked without incident throughout that day. Sure enough, I was late again the next day. But I was glad it was payday Friday, and I'd be able to fix my tire, pay some bills, get some rest, and be fresh and ready to work on Monday. Suddenly, while on a call, and without any notice, I began to cry. I don't know why but tears starting streaming down my face faster than I could wipe them away. I finished my call, went to the bathroom and cried uncontrollably for an hour. When I finally came out, my boss said, "Zina since you can't separate your private life from your work, I'm going to have to let you go". I was livid. I couldn't believe he would fire me after everything else I had gone through over the last couple of days. I was pissed that he would fire me knowing that I had walked to work. He knew the day before that he was going to fire me. Why have me walk to work two days in a row. I felt like a fool and I refused to leave.

I told him he could either find me a ride home or call the police because I was not walking back home. After calling security and having the office administrator come over and take me out of the building, I continued to rant and rave outside of the front office until the CEO came out. He asked me why I was so upset and I told him the whole story. He told me I was right that they could have, at least, let me go the day before but he could not get me my job back. He gave me a ride home and wished me good luck.

At home, in the middle of the day, I didn't know what to do next. I sat and I cried for hours. With my last check, I was able to fix my car, pick my children up from school, and get dinner. I stopped along the way and got dinner and $50 dollars' worth of dope. I knew that I needed to stop doing drugs long enough to get the rest of my life together. But first, I was going to get good and high, then do a lot of praying that things would get better. I split the $50 piece of dope in half, put on some soft music videos, then calmly and quietly smoked the first half. I cooked dinner, bathed the kids, read them a story, then put them to bed. I set up everything so I would not have to move until I was done. It took me until daylight to finish the rest of my drugs. When I was done, I cleaned all my smoking equipment and neatly packed it up, put it in a box and placed the box in the back corner of my closet. I took a cool shower, dressed, and prepared myself to drop my kids at school. When I returned I got on my knees, near my bed and asked God to please help me clean up my life. For the next 30 days I don't remember much about what I did except pray and cry. At the end of that month I registered with 3 temp agencies and began working temporary jobs. It was the beginning of 1984, I felt good, I had been faced with a dark place in my life and I came out without any assistance from anyone but God. I landed a job at the Long Beach Chamber of Commerce. I was the only Black girl in the office and they all loved me. Once again I was making good money, I was still getting county aid, and my bills were paid. All four of my children were in private school and my car was paid for. Life was good again.

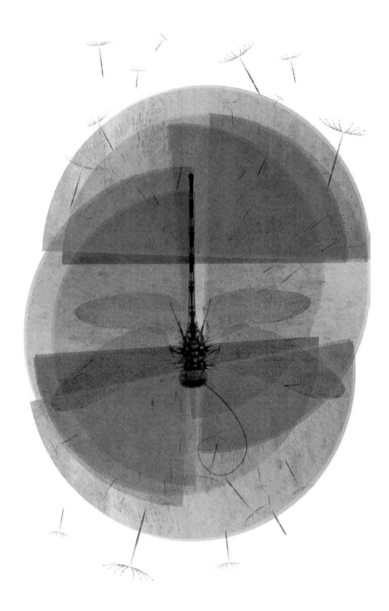

"We are what we believe"
C.S.Lewis

CHAPTER 7

Beginning To Look A lot Like Normal

I spent the year of 1984 living life like I was supposed to. I wasn't getting high or even drinking. I was taking care of my kids and being, what I considered to be, a law abiding, adult, citizen. An average day had me drop my children at daycare, go to work, pick up the kids, come home, cook dinner, bath the kids, and put them to bed before retiring for the night, just to wake up the next day and do it all again. Things had become so normal that I didn't even realize an entire year had passed by.

It was 1985, I was 25 years old, and I didn't feel like I needed anyone to do anything for me. I was living life by my own rules and I didn't have to answer to anyone. I was a little bored with the routine of going to work, taking the kids to the beach and the park, going home and doing nothing else. I bought a brand new car, the first new car I'd ever bought on my own. To break it in I drove some of the girls from the office to Palm Springs for the weekend. This was the life, I had arrived at last. I wasn't tripping off of Alvin anymore, Rondell had moved in with his second girlfriend since we had split, and I still hadn't heard from Terrance. I had talked to Theodore a couple of times but he had no plans to come to LA anytime soon. Rhonda was still modeling, Rose and J.T. were raising their family, and I was only in contact with Sheena on occasion. Since I had taken a break from doing drugs I wasn't talking too much to Teresa or Stephanie. I had become closer with Teresa's older sister Yvette. She would keep me up to date on what was happening with her side of the family. My younger sister, Wanda was on her own, working at the post office and raising her young son. Alicia was living a life more like mine. She was getting into some small trouble and moving in with different family members, my dad and his mother included. Just trying to find her own place in life, I guess. Jack was still home with my

124

mom and my stepfather was still begging my mom to take him back, since they had divorced a few years earlier. I had not seen my other brothers since I left Chicago in 1979, but we talked often. For me, things were going much too smooth, it was time to put some drama in the game. I had only dated a little and I really wasn't interested in finding a man. I was, however, becoming concerned that I might be getting bitter towards men; I didn't want that. I decided that I would not marry again until my kids were grown and anyone I dealt with would have to accept me on a non-serious basis. I would not accept or offer any commitments. If I thought that they were falling in love with me I would end all contact immediately. I was not going to look for a man. I would just live my life and if a man appeared, who could handle the conditions, I would not turn him away.

I stopped for groceries, coming in from work one day. All the kids were asleep and I wasn't sure if I should take the kids in first or the groceries. I was just sitting in my car trying to catch my breath for a minute. I decided that the kids were heavier and I'd better carry the groceries in first so I would still have the strength to bring the kids in when I was done. I opened the hatch door to my wagon and grabbed the first few bags and headed for the house. He seemed to come from nowhere. "Please, may I help you beautiful, African queen." Stunned and flattered, I turned to face an extremely handsome creme colored, oval eyed, well built, smiling angel with out-stretched hands. Not wanting a stranger, however fine, in my house I declined. In a thick Jamaican accent, "won't you please allow me to give you a hand?" "It makes my heart ache to see one so beautiful work so hard alone." The last thing I needed right then was a man to deal with. I don't know where I found the strength, but I declined. But this is where it all began. He was staying at the art store next door to me, so I saw him almost every day. He would always offer to help me with whatever I was doing and I always declined. One day, after getting the kids and my grocery's in the house, they all wanted to go outside. Since it was still light out, I said OK. Once dinner was on I noticed how well the kids seemed to be playing with one another. They had never done that before. All I could hear in the kitchen was them outdoors giggling feverously. So I decided to check on them. When I got to the window I was astonished. There he was playing in the grass with my children. No cares about getting his clothes dirty, or messing up his hair, or getting down on his hands and knees, chasing them around the yard. It was a precious site. I stood there watching from the window. My children were happier than I had seen them in a long time. It dawned on me that I really needed someone around that could give them the nurturing they needed. I couldn't do it, I had to work, make sure the bills were paid, and that they a decent dinner on the table every day. There was no time for the truly fun stuff that kids needed. I had been alone for a little while now and I could tell that it was time to bring in someone to help my family feel complete. I returned to finish dinner, allowing them to enjoy their new found friend a little longer. When dinner was ready, I went out to call them all in and I thought I would burst at the site of what I saw outside. There he was, this stranger, turning in circles in the grass. He had a twin under each arm and one son to each side, swinging all four of them around until they were just delirious with laughter. When I yelled for them, he stopped and all five of them fell to the ground laughing until they cried. I had to go and retrieve each child individually because they were all too weak to walk. With the last one in hand, I thanked him for spending a great afternoon with my children and told him goodnight. "Goodnight, Ms Beautiful, African, Queen." I smiled as I closed the door to the precious angel who would remain on the other side. Cedrick, DaWayne, Shawna, & Keyanna ate without incident. Because they were so exhausted from the day, there was no argument when it was time for baths and bed. They all readily went to bed and were asleep before I could leave their rooms. I sat in my room watching music videos, being extremely bored. It occurred to me that it didn't make sense for me to be sitting at home on a Friday night, especially with a sexy Jamaican right next door. I decided I would go sit and talk for a while, find out what this guy was all about. As soon as I turned the building corner, it startled me to see him sitting right in the door way. He had an art table in the doorway and he was working on this weird piece of art. Because I wasn't expecting him to be sitting there, I jumped. Feeling silly, I began to laugh. Unsure of what was so funny, he began to laugh too. It was a great ice breaker. "Why Ms African Queen, whatever is so funny?" I told him why I was laughing then took a seat at the table. I said, "Hi, my name is Zina." He said, "My name is Harold, it's nice to meet you." He was molding this clay man and asked me how I thought it looked. I told him that the eyes were crooked and that he should take them off and put them on again. So he did and the eyes would not stay on after that. We laughed so hard, we cried. When the laughter died, he was staring at me intensely. It made me a little uncomfortable and to break the tension I asked if he smoked weed. I already knew the answer because his eyes were so tight, I could hardly see them. His smile broadened when he replied, "I always keep a little of the gungi man, do you indulge?" "Sure I do, do you have any left?" And so it began. We smoked and laugh into the night and I had made a friend for life. It didn't matter if we never got together but I knew I wanted him to be my friend from now on. I thought it odd that he was a Jamaican named Harold but that night I found out he wasn't

Jamaican. Harold was from Pittsburgh. His last girlfriend out there was from Jamaica. His accent was fake. Harold had only been in California for a short time and was just beginning to get on his feet. He had a twin who died from his appendix bursting when they were only 21 years old. I'm sure that was a very traumatic experience for them. Harold had a brother named Jim who was married to a Samoan named Talia. They had two sons. Harold lived with his cousin, who was a vegetarian and would not allow any meat in his house. He hated living with him because he was treated like a child, and was not allowed to run his own life. Harold was 30 years old and had been very lonely since he came to California. He was not working and couldn't offer a woman a date. Before the night was over, I told him that I had become very lonely as well and couldn't find anyone that I felt comfortable with around my children. Since we were both lonely, we decided to keep each other company until we found our true mates. Since we had already decided we would not be together seriously, we didn't see the need to wait before sex. So, it happened that night. Not having gotten high in about a year, I was so wiped out that I fell asleep. I woke up, this summer morning, to the sound of my children crying, not knowing where I was. I was so ashamed, I didn't even want to go outside. I didn't want my children to know I had left them overnight to spend the night with a man. Harold told me he would go and get them inside so I could clean up and look presentable. He'd tell them I went to the store. I agreed, got up, got cleaned, and ran to the corner store and bought sugar. When I returned, Cedrick told me I should never do that again, because it scared them and they thought something had happened to me. Even though they were very young, they knew it was not normal for me not to be home when they got up each morning. They knew that I had done something very bad and they wanted me to know just how bad it was. I agreed and apologized for scaring them that way. I assured them that it would never happen again. We went through the day without incident and Harold spent the day with us. We played around the house and a little in the yard. The kids really enjoyed having Harold around. It was a good day. I was surprised to hear one of the kids tell Harold that he should live with us. I told them that he couldn't live with us but that he could spend the night if he wanted, (and of course, he did). With all the problems he had been having with his cousin, I didn't want him to go back to that. He was such a nice guy, he shouldn't have to live like that. Nights, turned into days, days into weeks. Finally one day his cousin told him to come pick up his things. Now he really had nowhere to go and I felt responsible. Since it was my fault I told him he could stay with us for a while, until he got on his feet. No one could have told me then what was to come for Harold and me. No one could have told me that things would get ugly, that we would grow to despise one another or that we would wind up full blown crack-heads. I would not have believed it.

It was cool having Harold there. He took very good care of my children. He cooked and cleaned while I worked. We had a very nice setup until people began to think we were an item. I don't know what I thought we were doing but I didn't want other people to think I was taking care of this grown man. I began to focus on all the negatives about him. I started to pressure him about finding a job. I hadn't said anything before.

But now, all of a sudden, I thought I needed him to work. It was never about him or even us. It was about what I didn't want others to think. Thinking back on it today, it could have worked very well, but I made sure that would never happen. Things were getting a bit too serious for me. I knew I didn't want to marry anyone before raising my kids and I certainly was not going to let my heart get in the way of that. I began to remind him of our agreement at the beginning. That we were just "friends". That he was free to date and so was I. He told me he had no desire to date. I let him know that I would do whatever I pleased, and that he was not my man and could not control me. I was determined to live carefree, not having to answer to anyone. I would never let anyone dictate to me how I should come and go the way Rondell did...especially not Harold. I became very irresponsible, going out often and staying out late. I thought that if he felt I was just using him as a baby-sitter that he would leave. But he remained faithful. I even started seeing other people hoping he would go away, but that didn't work either. Soon I begin to enjoy the freedom I had. Being able to go out and come home

133

without an argument. I became accustomed to this dysfunctional behavior, (and so did he). He didn't care where I went as long as I came home. That would be fine for a while but I knew I had to find a way to put some distance between us. I just wasn't sure how to make that happen.

Just a few short months later, I got my answer. We were being evicted from our apartment and I wasn't sure where we were going to live. I told him that I was going to find someplace for my children and I and he would have to be on his own. I thought, finally, I'm gonna be free. I found a place that would not be ready for a month so me and the kids went to my mother's and he went to his brother's house. I had been talking to the Theodore for a couple of months. He was talking about joining the Marines and being stationed in San Diego. I thought about him a lot, especially since my divorce. I often fantasized about what life could have been like if things had worked out for us. The eviction gave me an excuse to get away from Harold so I could pursue a fantasy I'd been having since high school. I moved to my mom's and Theodore did boot camp in San Diego. As soon as he was done, I went to visit him. I couldn't wait to see him. I even bought a new outfit, I had never done that before, (and haven't done it since). When I got there I was shocked to find that he had not changed one bit. The previous five years had absolutely no effect on him. Even his hair was still red. It was as if not one day had gone by. All these years we had been talking on the phone about how we would begin life again once I was free. Now the day had finally come. We could begin our life together, the life it should have been all along. By the end of the day, I had spent enough time with him to know why he didn't seem to have changed since high school. It was because, truly, he hadn't. He was the same immature little boy I had left back in Chicago five years earlier. His personality was still the same, his attitude was still the same, and even his goals had not changed. Somehow, I managed to twist all that information and convince myself that he was just acting like that because he was excited to see me. Even though he had not changed, I had. My life was very different. I had four children to raise. Children that were not his. I drove to San Diego every weekend. Leaving the kids with my mom at first. The day came when she told me that she was not going to watch my children while I went out sleazing around. No matter. I just took them with me. Theodore began to complain about the condition of my kids clothes. Asking why they were so dingy? Why didn't they have anything new? He didn't seem to understand the concept of cost. Tiring of his constant complaining, I told him that if he didn't like the way my kids were dressed then he could buy them new clothes. That didn't sit too well with him. Again, I was faced with the reality of Rondell's prediction. Here was ANOTHER man that could not (or would not) accept my children as a package deal with me. As the nit-picking continued, the drive to San Diego didn't seem worth it as much anymore.

Not driving to San Diego every weekend left a lot of time for me to spend with Harold. We were on again and off again a lot. This time we were on again. I would pick him up on Friday and we would take long drives. Then we would return to Long Beach to our favorite parking lot. Since I lived with my mom, we didn't have any place to really be alone.

We would often take the kids on long drives up Pacific Coast Highway, along the beach, until they fell asleep. Once they were asleep, we'd head back to our favorite spot, an open Long Beach parking lot that faced the water. I would park on the top level and on a clear night we could see Catalina Island, we would all sleep there until the sunrise woke us up. Many nights Harold and I made love on that roof top. It was on that roof top one morning just before dawn that I conceived my 5th child. We got an apartment in Long Beach on Pacific Ave. But before I could give birth to the baby, we were being evicted again. The difference this time was that my Section 8 subsidized housing certificate had come through. It would just take sixty days before I would have my certificate in hand. Once I had it, I would have 90 days to find an apartment. The only condition was that the apartment had to be in LA. So at 7 months pregnant, I went to my mother's AGAIN, he went next door to my grandmother's. Before I received my certificate I went into labor.

"If I say, 'surely the darkness will hide me and the light become night around me', even the darkness will not be dark to you and the night will shine like the day, for darkness is as light to you"
Psalm 139:11-12

CHAPTER 8

Not As Normal As It Looks

On May 24, 1986, I gave birth to one of the most beautiful baby girls I had ever seen. Sabrina Monique. I was going to be 26 years old on my next birthday. Soon after giving birth, I resumed my search for a place to raise my family. When Sabrina was 3 months, I found the perfect apartment. A newly built 3 bedroom, 2 bathroom, with a laundry room, upstairs apartment on 111th and Main. It was on the east side of Figueroa. I didn't think much of it at the time but it soon became very significant. The east side of Figueroa was a very different world. A world I never knew existed, even though I had been raised in LA (and this place was only a few blocks from my mother). There was a mixture of houses and apartments on my block. There was also a mixture of home owners and renters. Home owners take better care of their property than renters do. Most of the home owners were elderly families whose homes were paid for. The renters consisted mainly of young, single parent households. We were not far from the projects of Watts, CA and you could tell by the mentality of the people (even the elderly). The neighborhood was sprinkled with gang bangers, dope dealers and all the "wanna-be's" that went with that life style. Additionally, there were respectable, middle class families as well.

My new landlord, Mr. Leland Black, had only 4 rules, keep the place clean, pay the rent on time, don't do drugs and stay away from the neighbors. I was reminded of the warnings of my mother years ago with Robin (the family that ran us off of Wilton Place and me to Chicago in the mid 70's).The family that lived next door reminded me a lot of the Andersons. Cat (her 4 kids), Fran (her 2 kids), Tracy (her 4 kids), Val (her 1 kid), and their gay brother Floyd (often with his gay friend) lived there with their mother (along with another brother who was often in jail). They had 2 cousins that visited a lot, Candy and Michelle. There was always some sort of commotion over there. I rationed that if I took my mother's advice this time and not associate with them, I should have no problems. I would receive strange stares from them as I came and went. Not wanting any trouble, I would simply speak and keep going. They were very taken with Sabrina and always wanted to keep her for short periods of time. One day, I came home from the store and couldn't handle all the bags and Sabrina too. Michelle asked if she could keep her while I took my groceries upstairs. Reluctantly, I agreed. When I finished getting my groceries, Michelle informed me that she was asleep and I should not wake her. After seeing that she was comfortable on a small pallet in the front room, I agreed to let her stay for a while. A couple of hours went buy and I went to retrieve her. When I got there, Michelle had personally pierced her ears. As outraged as I was, I didn't want to create an argument that could build into something big and long lasting. I simply informed her that she should not have done that without my consent, and never allowed her to go over there again.

Harold and I moved into what I considered a small slice of heaven (with the exception of the 80's version of the Andersons). Everything was so new that I only needed to sweep the saw dust from the cabinets and wipe down the dust in the bathrooms. My apartment was very comfortable, there was room for everyone. I enjoyed decorating my beautiful new environment. Buying curtains, decorative plates and glasses, as well as a new washer and dryer. Again, I had arrived and this time it would be different. I didn't mind Harold being there even though I insisted on reminding him that this was an arrangement and NOT a relationship.

I wanted to get back to the things that made my life familiar. Taking the kids on long drives, to the beach, the park and resuming my passion for the skating rink. Still smoking weed and having an occasional drink, I didn't see any problems with my life as I was living it. At the rink one night, I had been admiring a skater that was doing some things I wanted to learn. I ask him to show me some moves. Rodney Crenshaw did not hesitate to take me by the hand and guide me around the floor. This began a whirlwind romance that would go off and on for the next 10 years. Being fed up with the way she was being treated by everyone else, Alicia came to live with me. It was during this time that Sheena called to invite Harold and I to a Labor Day picnic that her, Michael and the band were giving in Long Beach. We packed up my kids and off we went. We had a wonderful day at the park that extended to Sheena's house at nightfall. Once we got the kids situated with movies, popcorn, and the like, Sheena summoned me and Harold into her room. We entered the smoke filled room to find one of the band members supplying everyone with what were called "primos" (weed mixed with cocaine and rolled like a joint). While this happened on one side of the room there was a mirror with lines of cocaine being passed around on the other side of the room. I wasn't too excited about the lines because back when I was living in Tanya's house (with her husband) he scolded me for sneezing over a mirror of cocaine lines. I thought he went just a little bit overboard for such a small amount of dope. I never wanted dope to be that important to me. But these "primos" were something different. This was a nice mellow high. Yea, I could do this. This was nice. Harold and I returned to our cozy apartment for a wild night of crazy romance. It hadn't been like that for a long time. He wasn't too happy with my involvement with Rodney, but he couldn't say much. Anytime he would make a comment, I would remind him that he could leave whenever he was ready. Alicia would come and go to her leisure, there weren't any real problems. I had planned a winter weekend trip for me and Rodney in Big Bear. A few months before we were to leave I found out that I was pregnant. Even though I suspected that the baby belong to Harold, I told Rodney 1st. To my surprise, everything in his response said he wanted me to have an abortion. I told him of my fears and that didn't seem to matter. HE wasn't ready for a family. When I told Harold, to my surprise he was very excited. Even though he knew the baby may not be his, he told me he didn't care. Harold said regardless of who the father was, he was willing to accept it as his and treat it as his own. I turned within myself. I had to ask myself some cold, hard questions. Could I deal with not knowing who the father was? Could I handle 6 children?

What if it is twins, or triplets even? Being almost sure the baby belong to

Harold and not Rodney, did I want to be tied to Harold with 2 children? I

already knew that one day I would leave him. What about the drugs? I

had been dabbling in "primos" since the picnic at Sheena's. Had I already

harmed my baby? Would my baby be born with drugs in its system?

With all of the bad decisions I had made in my life, the ONE thing I

always did right was take care of myself while pregnant. I was always

careful not to drink, do drugs, or even smoke cigarettes. In a whole lot of

fear I made my decision. I would not keep this child. I was devastated,

but I could not see myself 26 years old and unmarried with 6 children.

This thing with getting and being pregnant was out of hand, it HAD to

STOP! If I could not bring myself to bring this precious life to full term,

then I did not deserve to carry the blessing of life in my body anymore. I

will never take another life from God. If I went through with this

decision, then I would prevent having to make it again by having my

tubes tied immediately. This I did 3 weeks before Big Bear with Rodney.

On that frightful day, Harold begged me to reconsider and to not kill this baby. I simply walked out of the door and into Rodney'scar. We drove in silence to my destination. I hesitated to exit the car, he tugged gently at my arm. As I went through all of the paper work, I continued to be aware of the many opportunities to turn around. Being separated from Rodney and in the assembly line of women going through the many stages from the waiting room to the recovery room, I had what seemed to be an endless wait to just get this over with. Every few minutes the lights in the entire building would dim for a few seconds. After a long while, my gurney was wheeled into a room with 5 other women on gurneys. I lay there silent with tears streaming down the sides of my face one at a time. I knew it was almost time. One by one, the door to a room would open and a gurney would be wheeled in. As I lay there it dawned on me that the dimming lights were the thousands of blessed unwanted children being returned to God. Their life journeys being ended before having a chance to fulfill their purpose for being sent down in the first place. How many lives would be (or not be) affected by their absence. How many lost souls would wander the earth not knowing that the one soul that could have made a difference in their life was refused by the mother who could receive the blessing? Suddenly, the door swung open, it was my turn. I cried uncontrollably. The nurse leaned into me and reminded me that it was not too late for me to change my mind. I could still get up and leave with the blessing God had intended of me. Through uncontrollable sobs and slobber, I said that I was unmarried and the single parent for 5 other children. There was no way that I could care for another child. With her sad eyes being the last thing I saw as she put the mask to my face, it was only minutes before I was awakened. I was taken to another room, with other women who seemed to be comfortable with what had just taken place, where I was seated in a chair next to a bag containing my clothes. I sat waiting for the anesthesia to wear off when I saw it. It was a small single drop of blood on the tip of my right shoe. Right then the lights dimmed and the completeness of what I had done hit me. My soul cried.

I met Rodney outside and he seemed inappropriately cheerful. Asking me did I want See's candy, it occurred to me that he had no idea of what it took for me to go through what I had been through. If he thought See's candy could make it better than he was more ignorant than I thought. I came home to Harold who was waiting in the living room. He asked did I really go through with it and I replied "yes". He led me to the bedroom and lay me down to rest saying only that he was really hurt that I would allow Rodney to have the final say in the life of a child that both Harold and I knew wasn't even his. No one knew of the questions I had to ask myself. Not Harold, not Rodney. No one seem to understand that I make decisions based on what I think and feel, what they think and feel have very little to do with it. When it came to the children that I brought into the world, subconsciously I knew that I could not rely on anyone to truly stay BUT ME! I simply acknowledged that his feelings were valid and nothing else was said. A week later I had my tubes tied and in two weeks Rodney and I were off to Big Bear. During our weekend, Rodney got upset about me not knowing what I wanted for dinner one night. He stopped speaking to me and gave me the silent treatment for almost the entire trip. I couldn't believe that after everything I did to make sure we had a good time on this trip, this is how he was going to act. He didn't know that I made the decision to abort my baby with God and he didn't know that I had taken full responsibility of the decision myself. All I could think of is, that for all he knew, I had given up a baby for him. If he didn't appreciate me paying for the entire trip or if he couldn't excuse my inability to select dinner then FORGET HIM! I'd had enough. I was tired of men taking advantage of me; of taking me for granted, of taking my kindness for weakness. I didn't have to take this. I no longer cared if he ever understood how giving up my baby affected me. It didn't matter anymore. I had very little to do with Rodney after that. I was done. My feelings toward him changed forever.

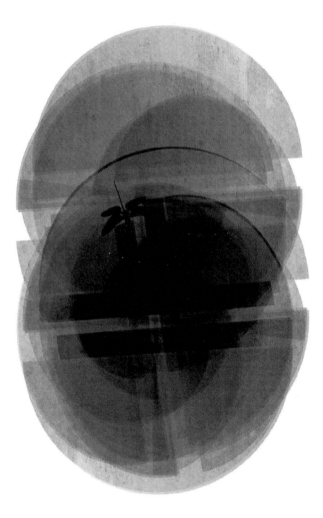

"Now the earth was formless and empty, darkness was over
the surface of the deep and the Spirit of God was hovering
over the waters"
Genesis 1:2

CHAPTER 9

The Beginning Of The End

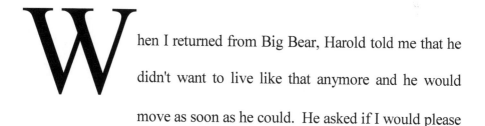

When I returned from Big Bear, Harold told me that he
didn't want to live like that anymore and he would
move as soon as he could. He asked if I would please
not see Rodney until after he moved. I agreed, not telling him that I had
already decided to not see Rodney again.

During this time it seemed that I had little patience with everything. The
abortion took everything I had left in me. I had been living in the fast
lane and my adult life had whirled past me in a flash. I was only 26 and I
felt defeated...like I couldn't win. Nothing seemed to satisfy me. The
kids got on my nerves, Harold got on my nerves, and so did Alicia. It

seemed like there was some strange whole in my gut that I couldn't fill. I couldn't shake the feeling that something was really messed up and I hadn't put my hand on yet. Me and Harold were still smoking "primos", Alicia was looking for a place and I had stopped asking Harold to leave. For some reason I just didn't seem to care about much of anything anymore. Whatever people wanted to do was fine with me. There was really no purpose for my life. The only thing I had of value were my children and I didn't put much value in that because I felt like anybody can raise some children.

It was the end of 1986 and Yvette called to say that Teresa was in trouble. She was living with a dope dealer name Barry Thompson. They called him "T". Yvette said that Teresa was being held against her will and that she didn't have anywhere to go to get away from this guy. I told her to give me the number and that I would take care of it. I called to find Teresa strangely whispering as if she couldn't talk freely. I asked her to come by my house and she said she couldn't. I asked could she have company she said only if she told "T" first. I told her to tell him that I would be by there on the weekend just to visit. Teresa told me not to be alarmed about the traffic through the house and that if I didn't feel comfortable, she understood. She knew that I had dabbled in cocaine before and didn't want it to be a problem for me again. I assured her that I would be fine and that I would see her on Saturday.

It had been a long time since Teresa saw my kids so I decided to take them with me to her house. The strange thing that I did before I left was pray. I sat in my room and I told God that I was headed to a den of sin and devastation. I told Him that I was going to rescue my cousin and I was willing to do whatever it would take to get her (and me) out alive. I ask Him to keep me safe no matter what happened. I even said that I may have to hit (the pipe) just to keep suspicion down if anyone was to challenge me or accuse me of being the police. I ask God to send His angels to protect me and my family no matter what I was to do next. Then I gathered my family and went to where Teresa was.

Teresa and "T" stayed in an apartment on the West Side. Me and the kids went up the stairway and knocked on the only screen door up there, it was barred. Someone asked who was it, I announced myself and then heard a series of locks being unlocked to allow my entrance. Once inside, a young boy showed me to a seat and spoke to a closed door to let the people on the other side know that I was there. After a few minutes, Teresa emerged from the room in a flower dress, gathered at the waste. She seemed small in frame but overall she didn't look to have been mistreated. She did seem guarded in her manner and almost pristine. She seemed so young and innocent, it reminded me of the catholic school Teresa that I remembered when we were young. I was suspicious because she had let that innocence go a long time ago. I wondered what had made her revert back to that place amidst all the insanity she had to experience running a big time dope spot. As I looked closer, her hazel eyes were red and her long, naturally wavy hair was much shorter than I remembered.

She offered me a seat at the table, I left the kids on the couch watching TV. She stated what I already knew was true, that it was not a safe environment for the kids and that I should probably not bring them again.

I agreed and assured her that we would not be staying long. She put some dope on the table and ask me if I mind and I said no. Before I left that day I took 2 or 3 hits and then I was on my way. While there, she gave me a little insight to her situation in the house. She told me that the way "T" kept her in check (besides beating the crap out of her) was to never let her out of the house without carrying something of value to him. Anytime she left his house she either had a bulk of his money, his jewelry, or his dope. He knew she would always return because she was convinced that if she left with anything of value he would find her and kill her. If he were unable to find her, he would find a family member and kill them. I assured her that if all we had to do was get her out of the house without anything of value to him, we would do it. Whatever it took to get her free, we would do that AT ALL COST!!! No one (including me) was to know of the Pandora's Box I had opened that day.

I went home that day and I told Harold what I had discovered. I told him what I was planning to do and that I would need his help. He would have to assume the full responsibility of the house while I focused my attention to the details of freeing Teresa. The plan that I had was to get in and get to know "T", gain his trust, get him to let Teresa out of the house with me and nothing else, then she would be free. It was a simple plan, I knew the stage, I knew my character, and all I needed was the script. I would make that up as I went along (life was nothing but a stage). For me, it was simply an undercover assignment. Harold agreed to help. I also told Alicia that she would have to move. I knew that things were going to get a little scary and I would not be at liberty to discuss what I was doing with anyone. I could keep it from the kids but I'd never be able to keep it from Alicia, she would certainly know that something was wrong. It was a little uncomfortable and I know she didn't understand why. I tried to reassure her that it had nothing to do with her, that it was just me but finally she moved.

I began to frequent Teresa's house on a regular basis. I got to know all of the smokers that hung out there. I got to know the various people that would come and stay there. I got to know who Teresa trusted, as well as who "T" trusted. It took a long time but "T" finally began to open up to me about different aspects of his life. I started to smoke frequently and carelessly. I thought I could control myself when the time came for me to stop. I would smoke with him and Teresa and bring up all kinds of subjects that would give insight on his character. At this particular moment I actually saw him to be a genuine good guy (I was wrong). As he began to take to me, he would give me a lot of good advice on how to survive on the street. How to determine who to trust. How to keep a straight face. How to pull off a good bluff. Barry (as I begin to call him) took to me so well that at one point Teresa accused me of sleeping with him. She said that he didn't trust anyone the way he trusted me (not even her) and under NO circumstances did he allow ANYONE to call him Barry. She wanted to know what had I been doing behind her back to get him to trust me that way. I understood her suspicion, I hardly recognized myself. It wasn't easy to live the life of a smoker and maintain an agenda under the influence of cocaine. My behavior under the influence wasn't easy to control. The craving for me was a lot stronger than it was when I tried smoking before. My appetite increased substantially in a very short time. I was becoming an addict (but I didn't know that yet). But I would always remind myself of what I was doing and why I was doing it. I had to remind Teresa of this as well.

In the 6 months that followed (it was spring of 1987), I encountered a great deal of near death incidents but I remained true to the cause. One time, "T" and Teresa were fighting and I began to beat on the bedroom door. I told him that I would call the police if he didn't stop. The door swung open and he had a sawed-off shot gun. He held it close to my face and said "he would blow my head off if I didn't get out of his business". Somehow, I talked him out of it. One day, he was so stoned out of his mind and he commanded his two large Dobermans to attack me. He called them back before they could get to me (for him, this was a joke). During another "smoke-a-thon" he threatened to throw me out the 2nd story window because I was getting too personal. Somehow, I managed to talk him down from that high also. There were many days where major drug transactions were being exchanged and many days where there was too much violence. But I kept my cool, stayed on point and by God's grace...I survived!

But I'd had enough. It was more than I could handle and I couldn't go on much longer. It was time to see if all my hard work was going to pass the test. One day I asked Barry if Teresa could spend the night at my house so we could go shopping the next day. He seemed a little hesitant at first but reluctantly he agreed. I was talking so fast that he didn't even ask for my address or phone number. Finally, my plan had worked. I told Teresa of Barry's willingness to allow her out and she became suspicious of his decision. Thinking that there was some sort of plot she almost didn't go. After some coaxing, I got her to agree. She packed an overnight bag, Barry gave us some dope to smoke, and with us grinning and waving, we said goodbye. We laughed all the way to my house. She was free. I couldn't believe it. It worked! When we got to my house, we sat at the kitchen table and I said "OK, Teresa, now what?" "What do you want to do?" She replied that she wasn't quite sure, that she needed to get some rest. We sat and chilled for a while, playing with the kids, watching some TV. During the evening, she stated she wanted to get something from the store. Without a second thought, I let her use my car. Hours later, she still wasn't back and I didn't know what to think, what to do, or even who to call. I certainly couldn't call Barry. I could call the police, but what was I supposed to say. Yvette hadn't heard from her either. I waited. And waited. And waited some more. Around 7am the next morning, she called. To my amazement, she was calling from Barry's house. She called to let me know that my car was all right. There are no words to describe my rage. After all I had gone through. After all I had risked. After all the times my life was truly in danger. I couldn't believe she would WILLINGLY just go back. She told me she would have someone follow her to my house to bring my car. I told her I didn't want anyone from there knowing where I lived, just bring my car and I would drive her back home. The operation was over and it was all for nothing. When she got out of my car, I pulled away from the curb thinking "I'll never come to her aide again". From here on out, she would be on her own. As I got off the freeway to return home, I had a terrifying awakening. Through everything that had gone on for the past 6 months, I had not noticed. Now, suddenly, it was painfully clear. I WAS HOOKED ON COCAINE. All along I thought I had a handle on things and when everything was over I'd be able to just walk away. The awful truth was that I was hooked and it would take a little more to get off than I thought. Up till now, Barry had been my only connection. No one in my neighborhood knew that I was smoking. In the course of everything going on, I encouraged Harold to smoke. It was the only way I could keep him at bay with all the time I was spending away from home. But he only smoked what I had brought home from Teresa's. I didn't have to spend a lot on what I smoked because Barry always gave more for what I was spending. To him I was "family". He never saw me tweaking, so I wasn't a "clucker". I always refused advances from him and others, so I wasn't a "strawberry". I usually came with some money (not much but some), so I wasn't a "freeloader". But now that the charade was over, my smoking would become my own responsibility. I had to find out what Teresa had told him about me. If she hadn't said anything about the plan, then at least I could still buy from him. The last thing I wanted to happen was for the people in the neighborhood to find out. Especially, my neighbors.

For a period of time, I was just a regular customer at Teresa's. Barry would allow me credit sometimes. My addiction took on an alternate personality. I began to smoke all day and most of the night. I started to make calls to Barry in the middle of the night. He reminded me that he generally only sold to dealers and didn't deal with a lot of smokers. He wanted me to keep things at a pace. To keep from letting him know how much I was really smoking, I began to cop from other places, so I wouldn't always have to go to him. I knew that one of Rondell's sisters (Annette) was smoking and another (Jackie) was dealing. I would go there every so often. My life was beginning to spiral downhill at a rapid pace. Faster than I could keep track of. All my thoughts about living life by my rules, showing my mother that I could take care of myself, proving to Rondell that he was wrong about me being a crack head, and convincing Harold that we weren't in a relationship, VANISHED! These thoughts were replaced with how to get the next hit. Nothing else mattered.

One summer night in 1987, being out of money and out of dope, I called Barry to ask for a $20 on credit. He told me to come on by. When I got there, he told me to have a seat and he would be right with me. There were about 10 other people there at the time, waiting to be served as well. Teresa was working another house not far from where we were. About 3 or 4 hours after I got there, Barry had served everyone else and they were all gone. He ask me to come to the room where everything was. On the bed he had hundreds of dollars in $20 bills along with some $50 and $100 rocks spread out all over the bed. On 2 separate dressers he had about 6 large bowl pipes lined up, all filled with resin. He was holding a pipe just as big, filled with just as much resin. He took one of the rocks on the bed and put the entire thing on the pipe he was holding. It was at this point he turned to me and asked "wassup". I suspected that from the unnecessary wait, I was being set up. When I walked into his room, I knew. I took everything he had taught me about bluffing and brought it to the forefront of my mind. I even took a moment to pray for the strength to walk if needed. I reminded myself that I was the actress and that he was the one who could be had. After all, he still didn't know about the plan that DID work. I said, "What do you mean Barry?" "I called for some credit, you said come on". Barry said, "Well ya know, my business has been a little slow, I really don't have any credit available right now". I asked him why he didn't tell me that over the phone. I had to be mindful to keep my cool. I had already seen him at his craziest. No matter what I thought of him, I knew what he was capable of. The last thing I wanted to do was piss him off. He told me that he didn't have anything for credit but that he had a business proposition he'd like to present to me. For a little bit of "oral sex" I could take everything on the bed. I asked "what about Teresa" He replied, "What she doesn't know won't hurt her". My craving strong and my head racing, I reminded myself that he couldn't SEE what I was FEELING. In a soft voice, and as calm as I could, I stated that those terms were unacceptable to me and if he didn't have any other offer, I would be forced to leave. Hoping that he was just testing me, I prayed that he wouldn't send me home with nothing at all. Just as calm as I was, he simply said "well then I guess it's time for you to go". It took everything in GOD'S power to get me out of that house. I never could have made it on my own. When I reached the freeway and was sure that Barry couldn't hear me, I screamed and cried all the way to my house. When I got home, I fell into Harold's arms and begged him to help me. I told him what had happen and how hard it was for me not to perform the request. I told him that I made it out without doing anything, but the hole in my gut was deep. The power of needing a hit was overwhelming. I clutched my hands closed. I grabbed my belly. Every inch of me was tingleling. My head was swirling and the room was spinning. I wanted a hit so bad that I ached. Even my hair folicles hurt. I was acutely aware of every pore on my body. I felt raw and exposed and the only thing that could quiet my senses was a hit. But there was nowhere I could get any dope on credit at that time of night...there was no hit in sight. I made it home but I would never make it through the night. Harold left me balled up on the floor crying. He turned on our shower. After getting me undress, he gently guided me into

165

the shower (still crying). With the warm water beginning to take effect, he began to lather me down. As I calmed down and my crying became soft whimpering, slowly Harold turned the water from warm to cool, then cooler, then cold. As I stepped from my cold shower, I felt better, I knew 2 things. I could sleep now and cocaine had me in its full grip. I also knew that if I continued to go to Barry's, one day he would get me to submit. I had to find a new connection.

The last time I went to Barry's, he wanted to sell me $10 worth of dope for $20 dollars on credit. I told him never mind, I would take my business elsewhere. When I turned down my block, I saw a guy that I often saw at the house next door to me. I stopped him and said, my name is Zina, I live in the apartment at the end of the block. I asked him if he would front me a $20 piece on credit for $40 on pay day. He looked at me a little strange, then asked if I was the police. After convincing him that it was a legitimate sale, he agreed. His name was Tank, they called him "Loc". This began a whole new phase of my addiction. I began to smoke in the neighborhood, it no longer matter who knew. My neighbors became my best friends. I smoked with Tracy most. Sometimes Val or Candy would join us (and Cat every so often). My life became really crazy. My house became a smoker's domain. I learned about certain smoke house rules from "T". I put them into full effect at my house on a regular basis. There was no way that my little county check would cover my habit, I would have to find a hustle. My house became well known on my block as the house of hospitality. Anyone who came to my place was always treated with respect (as long as they followed the rules). If they failed to follow the rules they would be asked to leave. It wasn't long before the crowd got to 30-60 people on any given day around the clock. It became known that if you were looking for a trick, you could come to me and I would hook you up. If you were looking for a "date", you could come to me and I could hook you up. I would rent different spaces in my place to couples for 15-30 min intervals. If you smoked in my place, you had to serve me in dope because I was the house lady. If I hooked you up with a "date" or a "trick", you had to supply the dope for the date as well as me for the hook-up. If you rented space in my place to smoke, I had to cop the dope. I would always get double up and serve dollar for dollar. It was easy to sell because I would sell in small quantities. I was the only place in the neighborhood who would sell $2 hits. The array of people that crossed the threshold of my place ranged from doctors & lawyers to laymen & blue collar workers to just plain smokers & crack heads. All were welcome. I had to smoke at ALL cost. I had lost all the respect of my friends and family. But most of all, I had lost respect for myself. It was the presence of all these people that allowed me to smoke in the quantities that I was accustomed.

My mother was at a loss as to what to do about me. She called my father and told him I was dying. He was able to arrange a small trip for his job and came out to LA. I cleaned up my act the best I could. But there was no way to cover up the weight I had lost. I was really thin and I looked anorexic. I managed to stop smoking the week before he came. While he was here I got a chance to see Wanda and Alicia. We didn't spend much time together anymore. They had lost a lot of respect for me because of the way I was living my life. They could hardly stand to look at me.

But they made an exception because our dad was here. One night my dad asked me to take him and Halimah for a ride. I drove and they both sat in the back seat. My dad asked me a lot of questions as I drove. Things like, "why was I smoking?" "Was it because of him?" "Was I ever going to stop?" I answered to the best of my ability and assured him that it had nothing to do with him. When I look back on it now, it's funny how he made everything about him. He couldn't even see my using drugs as something only connected to me. We went through the week without incident. The visit was strained but we made it through. I lasted an additional week after my father was gone. But then I returned to smoking again.

My mother ran into an old friend of hers, Ronald Waters. He had been someone from her past. I remembered Mr. Waters from when I was a young girl. He use to take us to the movies and to the park. He would always call me a little angel and kiss me on my forehead. I suppose he asked about me when he saw her and she told him of my condition. He told her he had some information for me and could maybe help. My mom called to let me know he wanted to come by and to get her off my back I agreed. Mr. Waters showed up with about 4 books regarding recovery. We talked for a short time, I thanked him for the books, and then he left. I skimmed through the books on occasion and even thought them to be somewhat interesting. But they didn't seem related to my situation to any great degree. The people in these books were severe alcoholics, I just needed to stop smoking cocaine.

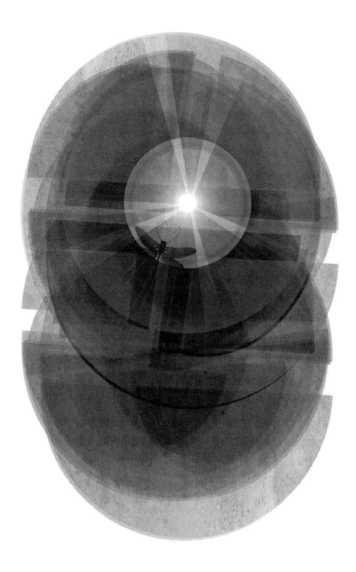

"The wisdom of the prudent, is to understand his way, but
the folly of fools is deceit"
Proverbs 14:8

CHAPTER 10

Darkest Before Dawn

I t was the early months of 1988. Up to now, my life had been moving at a fast pace in the rat race. I couldn't continue playing this role in the dope game. As with every stage play, at some point the curtain has to come down. The crowd had become too much for me to handle. My kids were often going hungry and unbathed. My car had been repossessed and the lights and gas were turned off most of the time. Paying bills and buying groceries seem to get in the way of smoking. I begin to try different ways to cut down on my smoking and cut back on the crowd. I even went so far as to tell people that I had quit. At some point I remembered some of the things my grandmother tried to teach me as a child. She use to tell me that if I were ever alone and there was nowhere to turn and no one to talk to, I could always talk to God and he would hear me. I begin to pray at night and read my bible. This allowed me to slow down to some degree but I still couldn't stop. Since I wasn't raised to live like this, I came to believe that everything had happened for a reason. That there was some strange purpose for the direction that my life had taken. I remembered how I had begun smoking again in the first place. I remembered everything that had happened with Teresa. It occurred to me that maybe I was on a mission from God and that I was supposed to fall into this den of iniquity to purge the pure at heart. So I started to read from the bible aloud to the people that smoked at my house. It took no time at all for the crowd to get REAL small. The only ones left were those die-hards who could handle debating about the bible while we smoked. Since the crowd was so small and my money had gotten so short, I often times would braid hair for dope dealer's girlfriends in exchange for dope. One day, I decided to use the extra hair I had accumulated to do my own. I spent all day and most of night to do my hair. The next day, I was so glad to be finished, I decided to show Carol (one of the dealers who had befriended me). She only lived a few houses down from me so I bundled all my braids into a pony tail and walked down to Carol's. One of the kids next door to her said she had gone around to Brandy's house (another smoker parent that Carol had befriended) and that she was really angry. When I got to Brandy's house, which was just around the corner, Carol was gone. Brandy's door was wide open and she was on the phone with the police. She was telling them that Carol had just left. She told them that Carol had beat her up and endangered her kids, and that she wanted to press assault charges. When I stepped onto the porch, Brandy just continued as if I had been there all along. She went on to tell the police that Carol was using all of the children in the neighborhood to transport drugs in Excedrin bottles. She stated that Carol had used her children and the children of another woman around the corner, Zina. I asked Brandy why she was lying to the police that way and she started to scream hysterically, as if I was attacking her. She started saying "GET OUT, GET OUT, HELP, and

SHE'S ATTACKING ME". I snatched the phone from the wall and tried to get her to calm down. I told her that she was out of control and I was sure that Carol was trying to help. Carol had already been discussing getting Brandy into a drug program because she had gotten way out of hand, she was putting her children in danger, smoking around them & leaving them home alone. Brandy had 2 children, an 8 year old son and a 5 year old daughter. Brandy screamed that I was there to distract her because Carol was coming back (I knew that paranoia had set in & she would not believe anything that I said). She started screaming for me to get out of her house. Feeling helpless, I turned to walk out and I heard a noise. I turned back to find that she had lifted the glass from her small end table and had hurled it at me, running right behind it. Using my arm, I was able to keep the table from hitting me but Brandy was right up on me. I began to swing. I didn't want to hit her or to hurt her, I just wanted to get out. As I was blocking her swinging at me I stepped back and stumbled out of the front door. When I regained my balance, her children were kicking and screaming at my feet. In my mind, all I could think of was what is happening here, how in the world I got in this fight, I just came around here to help. I was trying desperately not hit these little children who were just as hysterical as their crazy momma and I just wanted to get away from all of them. I heard Brandy screaming, it seemed to be off in the distance, but it wasn't. I looked up and she was right there. CRACK!!! I wasn't sure what had happened, then my face began to sting. My vision became blurry. I didn't know what had happened for sure but whatever it was, I sure had a lot of blood on my shirt. I knew I hadn't swung at anything. Then I saw it. Brandy was holding a bloody, glass vase. I was hit in the face. Brandy was screaming something, I don't even know what it was. I could see her mouth moving but I couldn't hear any words. I was in shock. Everything seemed to stand still. All of a sudden she wasn't hysterical anymore. I just walked around her and headed down the street. I slowly turned the corner still in shock at the amazing turn of events. All these people were crazy. Everything I had encountered since arriving to the east side of Figueroa seem to happen in a vacuum. I met people that had 5 generations of family raised in the same house. There were parents and grandparents that had children while still in their teens. Now their children were having children during their teens. It was a viscous cycle of recycling behavior patterns. A lot of them were involved in gangs. There were fights, shootings, jail time and teen pregnancies and it was looked upon as normal. It never reached the news, no one knew, and no one ever left. There seem to be this huge square vacuum of community that no one came to or left from. There were generations of families that had NEVER left the neighborhood their entire lives. How was that possible? How is it possible that you can't even help someone without winding up in some insane street fight for nothing, about nothing? I arrived at Carol's house before I got to mine. She was sitting on the porch with some other people. When she saw me she shouted my name. I don't remember hearing her or seeing her run to the edge of the gate. I just remember her asking "what in the hell happened to you?" I told her I went to Brandy's to keep her from hurting Brandy and I wasn't sure what happened after that. Carol said "I go to Brandy's house and beat her down for an hour and you go there for 5 minutes and get your face all jacked up" I asked was my face really bad and she lead me to her bathroom to clean up before my kids saw me. It created 2 large gashes. Looking at my face in Carol's mirror, seeing past my skin, flesh, and muscle and looking into the hole in my bone, I screamed God's name to the top of my lungs. I cried out for him to help me. I screamed, not because of any pain but because of all the anger. I had murderous anger and I thought I would explode. I wanted to murder her and I knew I could not live nor smoke that anger away. I stood there in Carol's bathroom and I cried, prayed, and spoke in tongues. When my spirit was calmed I went home and called my sister Alicia (who was pregnant) to take me to the Martin Luther King (killer king) hospital. I sat there trying to explain to my sweet baby sister what had happened to me. She and Wanda both tried so hard not to give up me. I looked so bad though, it was hard not to feel as though there was no hope for my return to a normal life. Wanda had long since lost all respect for me. She stopped speaking to me altogether (thank God none of my brothers would ever have to see me in this condition). In the midst of my explanation, a doctor ran into my room next to my bed with an exposed needle asking, "Who is Zina Stepter". I asked him why he was moving so fast with that needle and he replied "I don't have time to play Ms Stepter". "If you don't want stitches just let us know and we'll bandage you up and send you home." They bandaged my 2 holes up and I went home.

Two weeks later, I had a spiritual experience when in a fight with Cat for my dope, my wounds were reopened. I lay there on the ground looking up into Cat's face. She was holding a broken bottle over my heart. She was really angry that her mother would loan me money but wouldn't loan her any. For this reason she felt I owed her some dope. I could tell she was sprung & crazed. The look in her eyes reminded me a lot of Brandy on that day not too long before. Cat said she had what it would take to cut my heart out right there in the alley. My body went limp. I didn't care anymore. I didn't have the energy to keep fighting this fight. Not the fight with Brandy or Cat or anyone else in the game. I didn't have what it took to keep fighting this dope game. This street game. This game of "LIFE

IN THE FAST LANE"! I couldn't come up with the script, the stage, the character, or the play anymore. I knew I could not go on like this. I knew I could not survive the street life. All I could say to her was "you could take my life right now and my soul will go to heaven. I will sit at the foot of the father. I would even ask his forgiveness of your soul. But you would carry the weight with God the father for all your days here and in the hereafter, for taking my life before I had fulfilled His purpose (I thought of my baby). My prayers are with you." With a strange silence in the air, even with the crowd surrounding us in that alley, I felt her lift off me shouting, "THIS GIRL IS CRAZY". Her sister drove me to the police station to make a report, because THEY wanted her off the street. I had no intent on making a report. I knew what had happened to me. I had removed myself from the protective grace of God. This left unprotected me in a world of demonic evil. It wasn't the fault of these people that they lived the way that they did. It was the devil. I began to pray like only the dying can. Day and night, night and day. I prayed when I smoked and when I didn't smoke. I prayed on the way to the dope house and on the way back. I asked repeatedly for God to help me with my life. I begged God to rescue me from the hell hole I had dug for myself. It was here that I remembered the prayer I had prayed before going to see Teresa that day. I reminded God that I believed he would keep me safe. And I felt it. I knew. Help was surely on the way. I needed only to be ready to accept it when it arrived.

And arrive it did. Not long after I began this prayer process, my "Eskimo" showed up. I was sitting around the square "round" table when I heard the gate open. It was my mom's youngest sister Lanee. I had always looked up to my Aunt. She was only a few years older than me and she was living the life that I had always wanted to live. She had gotten saved when she was in high school. She had gone on to college where she met her husband. They married, traveled for 10 years, bought a house and a van (to add to my Aunt's VW), and then had 2 children. They even put the children's footprints in the cement by the garage in the back. She had a real "Leave it to Beaver" life. Lanee didn't have any experience with drinking, using drugs, promiscuity, or even cigarette smoking (nothing like me). She came to my door and rang the bell. In fear, I didn't answer. She began to knock. I hoped that if there was no answer, she'd give up and go away. She continued to knock. She shouted, "Zina, I know you're in there and if you don't open up this door, I'm gonna start spreadin' the blood of Jesus all over this building". The last thing that I needed on this beautiful Saturday afternoon was my aunt outside, spreading the blood of Jesus all over my building. I told her to hold one minute. There were only a few people sitting at my table. I dealt out a hand of cards so it would look like we were playing a game. I told everyone to just look "natural". I expected that when she saw me she would have that familiar look in her eye. That look that I had been getting from all the people that knew and loved me. That look of disgust at what I done to my life. That look of disappointment I saw so often in my mother's eyes. That look of disgrace I saw in Mr. Black's eyes. That look of shame that I saw in my father's and Wanda and Alicia's eyes. That look that I had grown to hate and despise. When I opened the door that day, I got something I didn't expect. Lanee saw me, grabbed me, and held me close. She began to whisper in my ear that she loved me and that she could help me. She told me that if I wanted her help, all I needed to do was ask and if I didn't, just say so and she would turn and walk away. Up to now, everyone had been giving me ultimatums. My mother threaten to take my kids, Mr. Black threatened to evict me, my neighbors threatened to call the police. No one had given me any choices. Now I didn't have any real choices, but I needed to think that I did. I needed to think that if I wanted to, I could just say no thank you, I don't need your help today. My aunt gave me that. I sank in her arms and said, "Please help me, I don't know what happened to my life".

It's the summer of 1988, I'm 28 years old and every Wednesday, for the next few weeks, Lanee would pick me up and take me to Crenshaw Christian Center church for a Cocaine Anonymous meeting. There was praise and worship singing, prayer and scripture reading. The 1st time I went I felt good being in the environment even though I felt out of place because I looked so bad. But no one focused on that. Everyone seem to welcome me. I thought it was really nice for these Christians to make me feel so at home. It took me by surprise to hear during testimony service that those "nice Christians" were actually recovering drug addicts. It was my 1st introduction to recovery. I didn't stop smoking, but I was never late for a meeting. I wasn't sure what the meetings were supposed to do. I thought that maybe each week as they prayed for us, we would get stronger and stronger and one day I just wouldn't want to smoke anymore. So I showed up each week waiting for that to happen. When I went home and still wanted to smoke, I figured that the prayer hadn't been answered yet. One day Lanee was supposed to take me to a place in Lynwood that would refer me to a recovery program. She came to my house, in a hurry. She said that she had a meeting and would not be able to go with me to the referral service. She would have to give me the $25 referral fee and the $2.70 round trip bus fare and I would have to go alone. An alarm went off in my head immediately. I'd never make it anywhere alone with money in my pocket. I'd never make it pass the 1st dope spot. Seeing the look of panic on my face, she handed me the money and said "this is not a loan, this is not a gift; this is an investment because I believe in you".

With $27.70 in my pocket and Lanee's words in my mind I set off to a whole new way of life. Something in me knew that my life would never be the same. I'm not sure if it was because of what Lanee said or her faith in me or the fact that I'd been going to the church but I knew something was different. The service referred me to a hospital recovery Center in Pomona, California. The night before I was to leave, I tried desperately to get high. I had an image in my mind of the day I quit smoking on my own. How I was able to take my time and smoke a $50 piece alone, without interruption. I had a feeling that I would not get the chance to smoke again. I knew something drastic was about to change I just wasn't sure what and I wanted to finish my smoking career with a blast. That was not to happen. I spent most of the night getting rejected by one dope dealer after another. By sunrise I had 1 hour before my mother would be here to pick me up. I was trying to scrape whatever residue from my pipe that I had left. The next thing I knew, there went the car horn. Mom was here and she was ready to go. I had not packed,

I had not woke my kids, I had not dressed, and I had not even showered. I told my mother I would be right down. I grabbed my kids and put them on some clothes from a pile that was in the middle of the floor. I threw on something from the mountain of clothes that had grown in my room under my window. Harold was supposed to go to Redgate Hospital, in Long Beach. He put a few things in a bag and off we all went. When we came downstairs, my mother had the usual look of disgust that had become all too familiar. She couldn't believe that I would take my kids and myself out of the house (where other people could see) looking this way. I ask was she going to take me or sit there and fuss. My stepfather began to drive. When we got to the corner, I took one last look at Harold (he was headed to the bus stop). I knew when I saw him again, we would be cocaine free and able to pick up our life in a better position than we had been in for the past 2 years.

The drive was long and unfamiliar. The tension in the car was thick and my kids were quiet. My mother and stepfather didn't say a word during the entire ride. Since Rondell had taken DaWayne a month or so prior, it was only Cedrick, Shawna, KeyAnna, and Sabrina. The 5 of us were in the back seat, Sabrina in my lap, Shawna & KeyAnna in the middle, and Cedrick on the end. I tried to explain what was about to happen. I told them that I had been sick with drug addiction and I was going to the hospital to get some help. I told them that I would have to stay in the hospital for a little while and they would be staying with grandmother.

We arrived at the hospital. The girls didn't seem to understand but Cedrick did. He assured me that I didn't have anything to worry about.

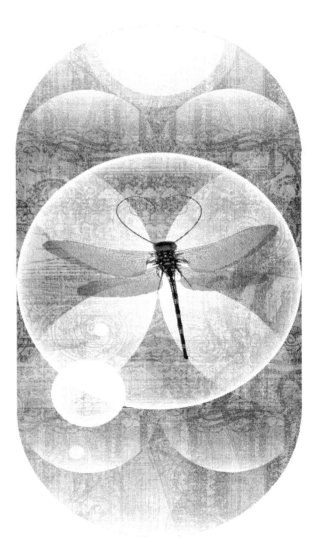

"While it is true that no one can or should live in the past, it is equally true that all futures are created out of the past"
Asa g. Hilliard III

CHAPTER 11

A New Outlook On Life

The lobby to American Hospital had tan couches strategically placed with a coffee table in the middle with magazines on top. Behind one of the couches was a beautiful indoor waterfall. The waterfall housed beautiful foliage and a small pond. The frame of the waterfall was an elegant winding staircase that seemed to lead to some other offices. On the back wall of the lobby were double doors that lead to a large pool area. It looked like a resort. I thought to myself, this is really nice. It's nothing like what I had heard from other people about recovery homes.

The kids stayed in the car with my Stepfather and my mom came inside.

We were asked into an office where a woman proceeded to ask me some questions about my drug use. Then I was asked into an examination room where I weighed in at 89lbs. Then I was asked to empty my suitcase for inspection. I asked could my mother leave the room and was told no. I opened the suitcase to a pile of unfolded, dirty clothes. My mother gasped and asked why I had not washed any of my things, I told her I didn't have time to wash. She quickly told the nurse that I was not raised that way and that I knew better. The nurse told her that it didn't matter, it was common and not to worry, there were laundry facilities on the premises. We closed my suitcase and the nurse told my mother that I would be escorted up to detox. She told her that she would not be able to talk to me for the 1st week but she could get a report from my doctor on my progress anytime. We returned to the lobby and my mom wanted to get her camera from the car to take a picture of what I looked like on my 1st day of recovery. The nurse told her there were no pictures allowed inside the facility. I suggested that we go outside and we were told that I was a "new admit" and if I stepped outside I would not be allowed back in. My mom went to the car and got my stepfather and my kids. They came into lobby, I hugged my stepfather and each of my kids one by one. I told Cedrick he would have to be strong and help my mother with the girls and he agreed. My mom began to direct the kids toward the door and reluctantly they started to shuffle out. One of them noticed that I wasn't following and told me to come on because we were about to leave. As they got to the other side of the door one by one, I stated that I couldn't come with them and that I would see them soon. It was the 1st time it seemed the girls understood that they were leaving and I was staying behind. They begin to cry and run back to the door. My mom, my stepfather, and Cedrick had to carry each one of the girls to get them into the car. I watched through the window as my mother drove away with my children screaming in the car windows. Just then the nurse tugged at my sleeve and said it was time to go.

We ascended the spiral staircase to a set of doors that led us down a long hallway. The intake nurse introduced me to another nurse and told her I was the new admit they were expecting. Just then a blonde haired, blue eyed white girl, running down the hall jumped to a sudden stop right in front of me. She said "Hi, my name is Audrey. I hope you brought your swim suit." I told her no I had not, I didn't know they had a pool. She said not to worry, I'd find one somewhere. She ran on, disappearing into a room not too far from where we were standing. The floor nurse told me she had to step away for a minute. She ask me to have a seat next to the desk and she would be right back. I sat there watching the different people come and go. Everyone seemed so happy. I wondered how long they had been there. The walls of the hallway begin to close in on me. I felt overwhelmed by something, I just wasn't sure what. I wanted to run but I didn't know where to go. Another floor nurse saw me sitting there and asked if there was anything that I needed. I told her that I was fine but I didn't want to sit in the hallway. I asked was there anyplace else I could wait. She led me into a room at the end of the hallway that had 2 beds. She told me that this would be my room and I could wait there for the 1st floor nurse to return. I thanked her and she left. Sitting there on my bed, looking out the window to the brick wall, I took a deep breath.

It seemed to be the 1st breath I'd taken for a long time. All at once, the severity of my situation seemed to cover me like a heavy rain. I thought about the previous few years of my life and wondered exactly what had happened. How did I end up here? I was 28 years old, I had 5 children (one who lived with his dad), I had no husband, I weighed 89 lbs., and I was a drug addict. All that I had experienced in life, all that I thought I knew, all the times I said "I'm grown, you can't tell me what to do", all the people I was going to prove wrong, added up to this. The sum total of my life came to a drug rehabilitation hospital. That was the best I could come up with. Had I lost my mind? What was I thinking? What had I done? What about my children, what did they think of me? I had to finally admit the truth. I WAS A FAILURE!!! I was defeated. They were right, all of them. My mother, my father, Rondell, ALL of them, they were RIGHT. I hated myself. The intensity was too much, too overwhelming. I cried the tears from years of disappointment, hurt, and devastation.

I was awakened, with a tear stained face, to a nurse who said I needed to have a tour of the floor. The first place she took me was to the kitchen. She told me that the patients had access to the kitchen anytime. The first thing I saw was an industrial sized refrigerator. It seemed huge, she had to tug at the door to get it to open. But oohh when she opened that beautiful door, my mouth dropped. In this refrigerator were the biggest, reddest, shiniest, apples I had ever seen. There was a big jar of peanut butter with a just as big jar of jelly. Everything seemed to be oversized, the milk, the bread, the juice, and even the butter. I felt like "Alice in Wonderland". It felt as though I could stay there forever. My two favorite places in detox were the ping pong room and the kitchen. From the kitchen we could see the residents down stairs. We were not allowed to interact with them, but it sure was nice to watch them interact with one another. After being in detox for about 6 or 7 days, I began to wonder what I would do when I got out. I knew I only had 10 days in detox and then I would be back at my place and my sobriety would be my responsibility. I was in deep contemplation one day. I gazed out of the window and watched the residents splash around in the pool. I could see them but not really. My thoughts were lost in a whirlwind of uncertainty. Suddenly, into my view, walked the cutest, darkest, most deliciously looking morsel of a man that I had ever seen. Immediately, it was clear what I needed to do. I didn't need to go home. I wasn't ready. After all, I would ONLY have 10 days, that wasn't nearly enough time to have any serious recovery. After only a couple of panel meetings, I thought I knew something about recovery. Actually, I had no idea of what was in store for me. I needed to go downstairs to the residential living. I needed much more time to get this thing called sobriety. I got up from the table and went to the counselor's station. I told the nurse there that I wanted to make arrangements to move downstairs. She told me I would need to interview with the intake nurse and I agreed. I had my interview on day number 9. The day I was scheduled to leave, they told me that they didn't have any beds available right then. I would have to go home, call every morning, and come back when they had a bed available. I would be required to remain sober on my own until I returned. I asked how long it might take, she said "2 weeks to 1 month". For the first time since coming into detox, the seriousness of my situation hit me. I told her I'd never be able to stay away from drugs that long on the street. She told me that if I didn't I wouldn't be able to return. I'd have to go back to detox and start over. She told me "the choice is yours!"

Reluctantly, I went home that day (it was a Sunday). My mom took me and the kids' home. It was strange being in the neighborhood, but I went inside and made a decision not to come out until it was time for me to go back. I called Redgate to find out how Harold was doing there. He had never checked in. On Monday, I called American and there was no bed available yet. I took my clothes out of the bag to wash. The kids and I slept in the living room because I was afraid to go into my bedroom and I didn't want to be alone. My room was the room I rented out the most. I didn't know what I would find in there. The next morning I called and there were still no available beds. I got up to finish washing, spend some time with the kids, and cook dinner. We watched movies that night. It felt a lot like it was before the drugs but I was on edge a lot. I just knew I would never make it the whole month without any drugs. The next morning I called and there was a bed available, I had to be back at the hospital the next morning by 8am. If I were late I would lose my space. Now, all of a sudden, the next morning seemed too soon. I wanted more time on the street, but that was not to be. That night I sat up with the kids and tried to explain that I would be away for a while. I told them that they would be staying with grandmother until I got back.

The next day my mom and I made the journey again from LA to Pomona. This was a very different ride than the first one. My mom and I talked all the way. I tried to tell her as much as I could about the kids likes and dislikes. I figured that it wouldn't be too much of a burden since she only had Cedrick and Sabrina. Rondell had DaWayne and twins. Two weeks didn't go by before Rondell dropped the twins off to my mother's claiming that he could only handle DaWayne.

This time instead of a suitcase with a bunch of dirty clothes I had 5 suitcases. One with coats and sweaters 3 with summer clothes and 1 suitcase full of books. The intake nurse told me I had too much luggage and I would have send some of it back with my mom. I convinced her to let me keep all but 2 of my suitcases. I had to send my coats, sweaters, dictionary, and bible back with my mom.

From the very 1st day in residential things were different than in detox. It seemed like two totally different places. In detox we could sleep all day. In residential we had to be up by 6am. In detox we could eat whenever we wanted. In residential we had 3 meals and that was it. There were mandatory groups we had to attend, conflict resolution, anger management, addiction education, etc. Our entire day was planned out for us from the time we got up in the morning until lights out at 10. Even our free time was scheduled into our day. That really cute chocolate covered morsel I saw from the kitchen window in detox turned out to be a counselor, Lionel Lincoln. Not only was he much shorter than me, but he couldn't have been less interested in me as well.

I attended my groups and did my best to stay out of trouble. There were 3 meetings that came to hospital, Alcoholics Anonymous, Cocaine Anonymous, and Narcotics Anonymous. AA was full of old people & NA was full of slow talking heroin addicts so I knew once I got out of rehab I would attend CA meetings (the crack-heads were the coolest of all three groups). After 30 days, I was allowed my first Sunday visit. My mom picked up DaWayne from Rondell's and brought all five kids out to see me. I don't know what I looked like in their eyes but it must have been horrific. As soon as they saw me running up to them they all huddled around my mom's legs and began to cry. They wouldn't let her go. Cedrick was the 1st one to come up and hug me. As he hugged me he began to cry and one by one they all came to hug me. We all stood there huddled and crying in the middle of the walk way. Once we got through that moment, we had a great day. When it was over, they asked me why I wasn't coming home with them and one more time I tried to explain that I wasn't well and that the hospital was trying to help me get better. In tears they all walked away. I cried myself to sleep that night.

We were required to attend Alcoholics Anonymous meetings on Saturdays, Narcotics Anonymous meetings on Thursdays, and Cocaine Anonymous meetings on Tuesdays. The AA meetings were populated with older white people. The NA meetings were populated with younger white people. The CA meetings were populated with young and middle aged black and white people. It was at these meetings that I felt most comfortable and enjoyed the most. I determined that when I left, CA would be the fellowship that I would cling closest to.

It was a hot Saturday afternoon when American was put on "lock down". Someone had gotten loaded on their pass and brought drugs and a weapon back to the hospital. Because of this the entire facility was put on lock down. Our morning activities were restricted to cleaning duties only. When our regular chores were complete, we had to take on yard duty until further notice. I felt irritable and edgy but I did as instructed until we were finished. At that point I was exhausted and just wanted to take a nap. The counselors however felt it more important to enforced mandatory PE time. We were required to play baseball. I requested to be excused and was denied. In my frustration I decided to leave. Much later in my recovery I discovered that I had a sore spot connected to baseball. Team captains never wanted me on their team because I simply could not play. It took a lot of journaling to discover this truth. But on this day

I just felt frustrated. I called my mother to pick me up but by the time I had packed all of the "donation" clothing I'd collected, I had changed my mind and wanted to stay. I had the receptionist call for Lionel Lincoln, after all we had established a pretty good counselor/patient relationship. When he got to the lobby I was crying uncontrollably trying to explain the events of the day and why it wasn't a good idea for me to go home yet. He listened and told me he would do what he could but that ultimately since I'd already signed the release papers it wasn't up to him it was up to my counselor, Matt. Since I was technically "AWOL" I couldn't have any communication with the other patients. I sat in the lobby and waited for Matt to come and let me stay. When he arrived in the lobby (with that smug look on his face), as humbly as I could I tried to plead my case. I apologized for my hysterical behavior, admitted I was wrong, and agreed to accept my punishment having to be benched for whatever extended period he decided. He let me get to the end of all my groveling before he half smiled, cocked his head to the side, and said "no Zina, I think it would be better for you to go on home. Maybe after you get loaded for a little while longer you'll return more willing to follow the program here without so much of a fight." I was shocked beyond description. I couldn't believe he thought I had gone through all of that just so I could go home and get loaded again. He pissed me off so bad that I made up mind right there that I was going to stay sober at least one year so that he would have to give me my celebration cake.

Afraid to return to my old apartment, I stayed at my mom's for a few months. I wouldn't leave her house alone under any circumstances. I would take the kids home on the weekends for a breather, since we were all staying in one room at her house. After a few months I knew it was time for me to be a big girl and go home. I packed up my family, thanked my mom for everything, and headed home.

While I was in the hospital, my mom, Lanee, and Mr. Black, all cleaned my house. It was almost as if I'd just moved in. It was just like new in all the rooms except my bedroom. My room was such a disaster that everyone refused to touch it. They actually closed the door on that room and pretended that it was not attached to the rest of the house. On my weekend visits, I would sleep on the couch. Now it was time for me to face many of my demons. I walked down the long hallway and stood outside my door for a long time. When I opened the door it seemed as though I could hear the screaming souls of so many people. It was deafening but I stood there determined to get through this moment. Unable to take it any longer, I stepped out and closed the door. I sleep on the couch again that night, determined to try again tomorrow.

I had met many people while I was at the hospital. Many who came to the meetings and made an impact on my life. One of those people was Jones. He was married to Barbara and I asked her to be my sponsor. While at my mom's I would call her daily to check in, but now I needed her in a way that I couldn't quite understand. This bedroom thing didn't seem like a big deal but it felt very much like a big deal and I didn't think I could get through it alone. I felt very foolish needing someone to help me get my room clean. But that was very much the case. Anytime I thought about going back to my room I would begin to hyperventilate. So I called Barbara and told her that I couldn't get my room clean. She asked me what the problem was and I told her that I had not done any laundry in over a year. In spite of the fact that I had a working washer and dryer, I had not done any laundry for over a year. The laundry had piled up so high and concentrated that it resembled a solid wall and could support the weight of any size human being. I couldn't determine quite where to begin. Barbara instructed me to go to my room and collect a hand full of clothes from the wall, close my bedroom door, return the hand full to the living room and proceed to sort, wash, dry, fold, and then put away the hand full. Only after this point could I return to the wall for another hand full and repeat the process. I came across many items during this process, paraphernalia, under clothes that were not mine, other things that reminded me of souls lost within the walls of that room. Each time I ran across something that would raise the ugly monsters from my past, I would call Barbara and she would walk me step by step until the article was safely discarded in the outside trash cans. Weeks passed before I was half through this wall. But there came a point when I experienced the presence of God. Doing my daily routine of gathering clothes, having coffee and watching television, I stumbled onto a miracle. I took a hand full of clothes from the wall, and low & behold there was fresh, plush carpet beneath. My bedroom curtains were open and the sun was beaming through. On the spot I had removed the clothes, sat right there in front of me a brand new, bright spot of clean carpet. I had finally made a dent in the wall. It was the first time that I understood the concept of perseverance and diligence. I understood what it meant to start on something thinking I would never get to the other side, then having the other side in site and knowing if I continued on the path I could reach my destination. In one single moment in time all the teachings of my mother, my father, my grandmother and my teachers came into full focus. I now knew what it meant to take responsibility for my actions and to maintain some discipline. For the first time in my life I understood what it meant to be "GROWN".

Because Harold continued to use drugs, I didn't know where he was. DaWayne was with Rondell.Cedrick, Shawna, KeyAnna, Sabrina, and I began our new life.

I had embarked on a new way of living and I was ready to take all that life had to offer, good and bad, as long as God was in front. But God HAD to be in front. There was no way I could embark on the journey ahead without God's help and guidance.

Through Alcoholics Anonymous, the 12-step program of recovery and God, I re-learned many of life's lessons that I refused to learn along the way. I've finally become willing to slow down and live life from a point of giving instead of a point of taking. According to the program of recovery, there are many wounds that must be re-opened in order to heal properly, but I'm ready for the task. I owe many amends to my parents, friends, and children for not being there during crucial moments in life. Whenever life becomes overwhelming, I remember the lesson I learned with the wall of laundry. If I'm diligent and persistent, if I stay on the path, and if I take only armfuls away from the pile, eventually I will see new carpet under any problem that seems too big to handle all at once. I can't change what has already taken place. I have, however gotten off the path of destruction I was on and therefore can change the future. I look forward to the journey ahead. I invite you to come along for the ride.

Forever found, Zina . . . THE BEGINNING!

54965481R00126

Made in the USA
Middletown, DE
14 July 2019

PROVERBS
THE

31WOMAN

TIFFANY CHEN

PR**O**VERBS THE
31 WOMAN

A WOMAN WHO FEARS THE
LORD IS TO BE
Praised

TATE PUBLISHING & *Enterprises*

Published by Tate Publishing & Enterprises, LLC
127 E. Trade Center Terrace | Mustang, Oklahoma 73064 USA
1.888.361.9473 | www.tatepublishing.com

Tate Publishing is committed to excellence in the publishing industry. The company reflects the philosophy established by the founders, based on Psalm 68:11,
"The Lord gave the word and great was the company of those who published it."

Book design copyright © 2008 by Tate Publishing, LLC. All rights reserved.
Cover design by Kandi Evans
Interior design by Amber Lee

Published in the United States of America

ISBN: 978–1–60604–625–8
1. Religion: Christian Life: Women's Issues
2. Religion: Christian Life: Personal Growth
08.11.20

Dedication

The Proverbs 31 *Woman – A Woman Who Fears the Lord is to be Praised* is dedicated to Jesus Christ, my Lord and Savior. He called me to walk on water and write this book in English, my second language. When I took my eyes off Him and began to sink, wondering if I could ever make it, He rescued me. He had shown me what to include in this book and the Scripture references that He would like to use, and when I was not sure of His will, He provided timely confirmation. Above all, Jesus Christ took my place on the cross and gave me eternal life. What amazing grace!

Table of Contents

Foreword

I met my mother many, many years ago one early morning in March. I don't remember all the details, but I have been told she was very happy to meet me. Fast forward some decades later, and I have truly grown to love and respect my mother. As a single mother, she worked impossibly hard to raise me and to give me everything I ever needed or wanted. Even when she was between jobs, there was not a single moment that God didn't provide for the both of us. I know now that was a result of my mother being a woman of prayer.

I would not be where I am at today in my walk with God if it were not for my mother digging me out of bed every Sunday morning and rushing me to get dressed for service. And if you have ever heard a ten-year-old armed with a violin, you would also know that my mother is a woman of true patience. She always took me to my music lessons through the half-dozen instruments I attempted to learn whenever and wherever they might be and somehow put up with my incessant whining about not wanting to practice. Today, I have headed up the worship ministries of a couple of different churches, my current being an urban church plant in the city of San Francisco.

I know my mother to be a devoted follower of Christ. She is a woman who truly seeks the Word of God and His righteousness. She tells me quite frequently that she prays for my future wife. I do not know a wiser or more faithful woman than my mother, and I can only hope that one day my wife will be as much of a woman after God's own heart as my mom. I hope this book encourages you and strengthens your walk with the Lord. May the Lord speak to you that you might grow into the wise and faithful daughters, mothers, and women He created you to be.

—Steven Chen

Introduction

Today's Christian women face many challenges: home, work, church, friendship, etc. They live a diverse and complex life style. Proverbs 31 describes the godly attributes of a virtuous woman who serves as the role model for Christian women for thousands of years. She encourages all women, regardless of race, age, marital status, and vocation.

The key to her success was her relationship with God. She was a woman after God's own heart. Her priorities were set by God, not herself or others. God was first in her life.

She submitted herself to her husband as she actively participated in their marriage as a partner. Her husband trusted her faithfulness and capabilities to run the family affairs. She was a loving mother who worked diligently to provide food, clothing, teaching, and finances for her family. Her children respected her.

This virtuous woman was a good worker. She got up early in the morning to do her tasks. If necessary, she stayed up late at night. She didn't just take care of the household responsibilities; she was also productive and profitable outside the home.

She was careful in her speech and the way she dressed herself. She had a gentle and quiet spirit that pleased God. She wore strength and honor.

This is the first book of *The Proverbs 31 Woman* series, and its focus is on the personal relationship with God. As I seek God's instruction to become a godly woman, I am encouraged to share this book with all the Christian women around the globe. May God be glorified through our lives.

The First Lady

In the beginning, God created the heavens and the earth. He then created Eve from one of Adam's ribs. It is the biblical truth that a wife is meant to be side-by-side with her husband, not above or under.

> And the Lord God commanded the man, saying, "Of every tree of the garden you may freely eat; but of the tree of the knowledge of good and evil you shall not eat, for in the day that you eat of it you shall surely die."
>
> Genesis 2:16–17

Adam told Eve God's command. But Eve had her historical conversation with the serpent and ignored her husband's warning. That conversation changed mankind; she sinned against God and also led her husband to eat the forbidden fruit. One small bite for a woman, one giant bait for humankind. Sin snaked into the world.

The Flood

It was Eve's fault that Satan and his associates crept into the world and worked overtime to tempt people to defy God's Word. God saw that the wickedness of man was great in the earth, and He was grieved in His heart. "So the Lord said, 'I will destroy man whom I have created from the face of the earth, both man and beast, creeping thing and birds of the air, for I am sorry that I have made them'" (Genesis 6:7). On the face of earth, there were only Noah and his family, eight people, who believed God and obeyed His Word. God established His covenant with Noah and instructed Noah to build an ark for the flood to come. Noah did exactly what God had told him.

All the righteous saints who have found favor in the eyes of the Lord obey His commands. I used to think that I truly obeyed God until He convicted me. One secret to obeying God is detail. One day I took off from work and planned to paint my house. I am usually restless due to my personality. The Lord said to me that He is not a God who would want me to paint the house on a vacation day when I worked for Him full time in the market place. Also, I had not had time off for a while.

"Go shopping in the afternoon," He said.

I proposed a second opinion: "Why don't I go shopping in the morning and then work around the house in the afternoon?"

"Do what I told you," He replied.

I waited anxiously. When it got close to noon, I checked my mail out of habit and found a 20% off coupon for the store that I was going to later. Since I was anointed to go shopping that day, God had put my name on all my blessings. The gracious heavenly Father can't wait to bless us, if we listen and obey precisely.

The Lord gave Noah specific instructions when he built the ark (Genesis 6:15–22). I am glad that he didn't seek a second opinion; otherwise, the ark couldn't have endured the flood, which would have been the end of human history.

Dr. Warren W. Wiersbe commented,

> If the cubit mentioned was the standard cubit of eighteen inches, then the vessel was 450 feet long, 75 feet wide, and 45 feet high. It had three decks, one door, and a series of small windows eighteen inches high right under the roof, providing light and ventilation. The three decks were divided into compartments (Gen. 6:14) where the various animals would be kept and where Noah and his family would live. This vessel was designed for flotation, not navigation. It was a huge wooden box that could float on the water and keep the contents safe and

dry. Dr. Henry Morris calculated that the ark was large enough to hold the contents of over 500 livestock railroad cars, providing space for about 125,000 animals.[1]

I wonder what went through Noah's neighbors' mind while he and his family were building the ark. The ark was so huge that even if they tried, they couldn't have ignored it. None of them had repented and turned to the Lord. They must have been laughing at Noah until the flood came and they couldn't laugh anymore.

Why did God single out Noah instead of his next-door neighbor who watched him build the ark? Noah believed in God and obeyed His Word. People constantly complain and resent the saints whom God has chosen to serve Him in *glamorous* ministries. The *glamorous* ministries only look glamorous. Are the whiners willing to do what those saints have to do to be in God's calling? "Jesus said to him, 'If I will that he remain till I come, what is that to you? You follow Me'" (John 21:22). Jesus Christ warned Peter not to be concerned with what He might do in the life of another. We are to follow Jesus Christ and mind our own business. God uses warriors whose faith has been thoroughly tested, not people who accuse, judge, belittle, gossip, and slander God's faithful followers. They fight against God, who strategically places His consecrated servants. God's promises for His chosen people are: "I will bless those who bless you, and I will curse him who curses you; and in you all the families of the earth shall be blessed" (Genesis 12:3). Wiersbe said that "God is love, but God is also light; and in His holiness, He must deal with sin."

How was Noah going to find such diverse animals, birds, and creeping things? God would lead these creatures to come to Noah and enter the ark. When we obey God to do our part, God will do His part, the miracle. God chose two of each kind of creature to keep, but how did He make the selection? We will have to leave it as God's secret.

I am sure He wouldn't have chosen my neighborhood cat. The cat would get into the garbage bags if I put them out the night before the pickup day. On so many cold winter mornings, when I had to clean up the mess before I made it to work by seven thirty a.m., I had envisioned the newspaper headline saying, "Cat Crucified By Its Angry Neighbor." The cat is still living today and messing with the garbage bags because I have found out that it belongs to the lady across the street; she is physically challenged. I sometimes walk around the neighborhood, and while I was there talking to her one day, the cat showed up. She asked if it had created any problem for me; many neighbors had complained. I swallowed the annoyance. When I work in the yard the cat often visits me, but I don't like anything that has overly developed social skills. Besides, it looks like the big fluffy *Rum Tum Tugger* in the Broadway musical *Cats*. I read Proverbs 25:17, "Seldom set foot in your neighbor's house, lest he become weary of you and hate you," to the sinning creature; however, there is no sign of repentance. I shall try baptism; water will work.

On the tenth day of the second month, Noah and his family moved into the ark as God instructed. Two by two, all the selected living things of every sort went into the ark to Noah. They were male and female, so there were no homosexual animals on board. A week later, on the seventeenth day, the Lord shut the door of the ark, and it started to rain for forty days and forty nights. The water eventually covered all the high hills under the whole heaven, and the Lord destroyed all living things. Only Noah and those who were with him in the ark remained alive (Genesis 7:1–23).

The water continued to rise for another 150 days, and then God remembered Noah. He then made the water subside and the rain from heaven restrain. It took another 150 days for the water to recede, and two months and ten days later, the earth was dry. Then the Lord opened the door of the ark, and Noah, his family, and all the living things left the ark—the triumphant entry onto the dry earth. They had been in the ark for a year and ten days. When Noah and his family went into the ark, they didn't know how long they were going to be there. But they believed that their times were in God's hands, and everything happened in God's timing and order. Noah built an altar to the Lord and offered burnt offerings, and God established His covenant with Noah that He would never send another flood to destroy the earth (Genesis 7:24, 8:1–21).

The Fire

God shall not send another flood, but the next judgment shall be fire.

> But the cowardly, unbelieving, abominable, murderers, sexually immoral, sorcerers, idolaters, and all liars shall have their part in the lake which burns with fire and brimstone, which is the second death.
>
> Revelation 21:8

We all have sinned. How do we identify true believers from non-believers? The former sin occasionally and repent to receive God's forgiveness; the latter sin freely and frequently and refuse to repent. Churchgoers and church staff may not be believers. Nobody is sinless; however, true Christians are completely loyal to God. Faith without works is dead. "You believe that there is one God. You do well. Even the demons believe—and tremble!" (James 2:19) Devil's associates know God, but they don't obey God. Joyce Meyer said that no matter how long a person *sits* in the garage, he will not turn into a car. True spiritual power is in meekness and gentleness (2 Corinthians 10:1), not in outward appearance (2 Corinthians 10:7) or boastful speech (2 Corinthians 10:10). In evaluating ministries or relationships, pray to seek God's wisdom, practice spiritual discernment, and be led by peace.

We all have suffered. How do true believers suffer differently from non-believers? The former suffer to share Jesus Christ's pain on the cross; the latter suffer for their disobedience.

> Beloved, do not think it strange concerning the fiery trial which is to try you, as though some strange thing happened to you; but rejoice to the extent that you partake of Christ's sufferings, that when His glory is revealed, you may also be glad with exceeding joy.
>
> 1 Peter 4:12–13

We don't rejoice that the Lord will judge the wicked sinners, but the righteousness and glory of our Lord will be magnified when Jesus Christ returns. Those who place their faith in Jesus Christ have their names permanently written in the Lamb's Book of Life. The rest of them will find themselves in the lake of fire (Revelation 20:12–15). "There is no God," will be a true statement there.

When Jesus Christ returns God will make all things new; *Your kingdom come* will be fulfilled. Apostle John describes in Revelation 21:1–5 that there will be a new heaven and a new earth, for the first heaven and the first earth will be passed away. The holy city prepared in heaven, New Jerusalem, will descend to earth. God will dwell with His people, and there will be no more tears, death, sorrow, crying, or pain. In this holy city, we will see God's face (Revelation 22:4). I always want to see what God looks like; He doesn't allow me to see His face when He visits me. My wish shall come true when I live in the most beautiful city with God and prayerfully all of you. I will hang around God and serve Him in our eternal home, where there will be no sun or moon for the glory of God illuminates it, and there shall be no night.

The twenty-first chapter of the book of Revelation describes the holy city being laid out as a square. Its length, width, and height are equal and made of pure gold, like transparent glass. The city has a great and high wall, made of jasper, with twelve angels at the twelve gates. The names written on the gates are the names of the twelve tribes of Israel. The twelve gates are twelve pearls. The wall has twelve foundations, and on them are the names of the twelve apostles. The foundations of the wall of the city are garnished with all kinds of precious stones. Revelation 22:1–3 says that there will be only one river of water of life in the heavenly city, and it will flow directly from God's throne in heaven. In the eternal home, man will have access to the tree of life, and there shall be no more curse. How magnificent! God is truly a God of beauty. Believers shall eagerly anticipate the Lord's return; the time is near.

If you don't have Jesus Christ as your Savior in your life yet, it is time to make the best decision of a lifetime.

It is not a coincidence that you are here. Life is difficult; I have lived it without God. I used to live in fear, not knowing what life would bring or if I would be able to make it. But God had mercy on me; He came into my life when I needed Him the most. Divorce and job change were in the same period of time, followed by my father's death. I was at the point where I had nothing to lose when I turned my life over to the Creator of the Universe, who loves me so much that He sent His only son to die on the cross for all my sins. Bow your head, accept Jesus Christ as Lord in your heart, and watch miracles happen in your life. God's faithful followers shall have double honor, and in their land they shall possess double. Everlasting joy shall be theirs (Isaiah 61:7). God's name is Faithful and True (Revelation 3:14). Trust in the Lord, He'll not let you down.

The Proverbs 31 Woman

A Woman Who Fears the Lord is to be Praised

How should we live as Christians to prepare for Jesus Christ's return? The first lady, Eve, failed to obey God; however, Proverbs 31 describes a virtuous woman who fears the Lord. "Charm is deceitful and beauty is passing, but a woman who fears the Lord, she shall be praised" (Proverbs 31:30). The virtuous woman does not deliberately disobey God; she pursues an ongoing personal relationship with God and completely surrenders her life to God. Men also can learn from her confidence in the Lord and holy living. At the Joyce Meyer Twenty-Fourth Annual Women's Convention in St. Louis, John Maxwell said, "When Jesus was born, instead of three wise men if there were three wise women, they would have asked for directions, arrived on time, helped deliver the baby, cleaned up the stable, made a casserole, and brought practical gifts; there would have been peace on earth."

Over the years that I have dedicated my life to the Savior, He has been patiently guiding me to develop a personal relationship with Him. The most important part of a Christian life is to know God and to fellowship with Jesus Christ in a deep way. Becoming a godly woman is a process; I am secure in God's unfailing love and know I don't compete with anyone else. I grow spiritually in His perfect timing and gracious ways. God spent years molding His servants for service—thirteen years for Joseph, forty years for Moses and Joshua, and ten years for David. I would like to share my blessings and encourage you to become all that God has created you to be.

Quiet Time with God— Pray and Study God's Word

The Bible is God's instruction book for life. In order to have a personal relationship with God, I need to learn the ways of Him. I have found the secret places in my home where I can spend time with God without distraction. It used to be a couch in the living room; later, God blessed me with a French country vanity table that I placed in my bedroom. I have a white woven basket in which I put Bibles, Bible commentaries, a Bible dictionary, other reading material, notepads, pens, and highlighters; I have everything I need when I study. Sometimes I spread out on the rosewood dining table for more space. In fall of 2007, I completed renovation of the den in the back of my home, and it is where I read and study God's Word now. I always begin with prayers, kneeling by the living room couch with my face in the pillow. This is where God has spoken to me miraculously during the critical times of my life. It is where I discerned that God had spoken to me about my mother's death. It was crystal clear that I heard from Him in my heart, and she went to the Lord three months later.

As soon as I wake up in the morning, I get on my knees to thank God for a day He has created and pray for Him to guide me through the activities of the day. I then study the book of Proverbs or Psalms. It is vital to begin each day with prayers and worship to learn God's wisdom for holy living. I make an effort to keep my morning study, even if it means I have to get up at four thirty a.m. Occasionally I have to make it up in the evening. Sometimes, I study other material God provides. During the day, I pray to seek God's will in all things; I am in constant communion with Him. A godly woman obeys God's will at all costs. Obedience is how you get to God's heart. A spirit-filled Christian knows John 15:5 by heart: "I am the vine, you are the branches. He who abides in Me, and I in him, bears much fruit; for without Me you can do nothing." All is vanity unless I am in God's will and He works through me to accomplish His purposes. God wishes to communicate His will to me; I need to put myself in the position to listen. In March of 2008, I started a thirty-minute Bible reading program in the evening that follows the principles in *How to Study the Bible for Yourself* by Tim LaHaye. Before I go to sleep, I pray and ask God to reveal my sins and confess them. " ... Meditate within your heart on your bed, and be still ... " (Psalm 4:4). This works better than sleeping pills. Wiersbe wrote in *Be Worshipful*, "Instead of tossing and turning in bed because of the things others are doing, take inventory and see if there aren't sins in your own heart that need to be confessed."[2]

I fast to study God's Word each Saturday. I usually get up at five o'clock and study a chapter of the book of the Bible that God puts on my heart. I always start with prayers and ask for insight to understand His Word. I use Wiersbe's commentary as reference. Like what it says in the commentary, Wiersbe brings the people, places, history, and teaching of the Bible to life. He remarked, "True theology (the study of God) is not a dry, impractical course in doctrine—it is an exciting day-to-day experience that makes us Christlike!"[3] When I study God's Word, the Holy Spirit speaks to give me wisdom and reveal God's will. I have studied Luke, Acts, Revelation, Hebrews, James, and 1 Peter. You need to study what God puts on your heart, though, instead of what I do. He reveals Himself to us according to our specific needs at different times. As I study God's Word, He fills me with His unconditional love to rest and renew my spirit, soul, and body. Time alone with God brings great rewards and a closer relationship with Him. I can hear God a lot better when I fast and invest time to get to know Him. Church activities can't replace personal quiet time.

Quiet time is not the time to give God my wish list and wait for it to be fulfilled. I used to do all the talking when I prayed and then walked away wondering why God didn't answer prayers. It is the time to be still in front of the Creator of the Universe and allow Him to communicate His will to me. When the Holy Spirit speaks God's will to me, I then pray accordingly. "Now this is the confidence that we have in Him, that if we ask anything according to His will, He hears us" (1

John 5:14). Some days, the Holy Spirit leads me to sing praises to Him. I also pray for the people whom the Holy Spirit puts on my heart.

"But seek first the kingdom of God and His righteousness, and all these things shall be added to you" (Matthew 6:33). Meyer said, "Making God first is the key to experiencing His best."

Besides studying the Bible, I also listen to great sermons. The Rev. Dr. Charles Stanley and Joyce Meyer are the two people who have made a major impact on my Christian walk. Shortly after God came into my life, He introduced Stanley to me; today I attend FBA (First Baptist Atlanta), the church he pastors, still read In Touch's monthly magazines and watch his teaching on TV. Stanley makes God's Word easy to understand because he fully comprehends godly principles. A new Christian needs to listen to the best preachers who don't just quote Scriptures on Sunday mornings. One of his books, *How to Listen to God,* marked a milestone in my life; I learned the various ways that God speaks and began to listen and obey. *The Extraordinary Life Challenge* helped me to assess where I was spiritually, financially, and physically, as well as set goals for an abundant life; it broadened and deepened my knowledge of God and brought me much closer to Him.

The first time I watched Meyer on TV, I became attached to her teaching. She applies Bible principles to everyday life. She is funny, down to earth, and full of life; she is a believer who has a personal relationship with God, not a religious Pharisee. God speaks through her so that I can enjoy everyday life. I have learned that

I only need to please God and don't have to meet other people's unrealistic expectations. I shouldn't allow other people to put me in their little boxes; I can be unique and free to live for God's purposes in my life. I have watched her TV programs, listened to her teaching tapes, and read her books. I admire her courage to be different. I am one of her partners and that means I go where her ministry goes, no matter if it is the prison or the African jungle.

How much time I spend with God depends on the season and the callings of that season in my life. God calls me to work in the market place, I find time here and there during the workdays to be with Him, and I study Proverbs or Psalms and read other books in the Bible daily. Each Saturday, I study the Bible, spend a few hours with God in the morning, and watch Stanley in the evening. Each Sunday, I go to church to worship and fellowship in the morning and watch Meyer and spend some time reading in the evening. I attended JFBC (Johnson Ferry Baptist Church) for about fifteen years; my fresh start of 2007 was to attend FBA. God called me to sing in the JFBC choir and later the FBA choir. "Whom shall I send? Here I am, Lord. Is it I, Lord? I have heard your calling in the night. I will go, Lord, if you lead me. I will hold your people in my heart." I answered God's callings by singing my favorite hymn, "Here I am, Lord," by Dan Schutte and Craig Courtney. When my son was little, I couldn't spend as much time with God because God called me to care for a small child, and I am a single mother. Pray for God to show you how often and when you should spend time with Him; it takes more than sixty minutes each Sunday to become a true believer.

The more I spend time with God, the better I can hear His voice. "My sheep hear My voice, and I know them, and they follow Me" (John 10:27). God wants us to understand His will; it is written, "The secret of the Lord is with those who fear Him, and He will show them His covenant" (Psalm 25:14). We need to know what the will of the Lord is (Ephesians 5:17) and do the will of God from the heart (Ephesians 6:6). Be a doer of God's Word. "And whatever we ask we receive from Him, because we keep His commandments and do those things that are pleasing in His sight" (1 John 3:22). When we walk in the light and pray according to His will, we will receive from Him.

> Not everyone who says to Me, "Lord, Lord," shall enter the kingdom of heaven, but he who does the will of My Father in heaven. Many will say to Me in that day, "Lord, Lord, have we not prophesied in Your name, cast out demons in Your name, and done many wonders in Your name?" And then I will declare to them, "I never knew you; depart from Me, you who practice lawlessness!"
>
> Matthew 7:21–23

Doing the will of God is a matter of life and death.

Tithe/Giving

> "Bring all the tithes into the storehouse, that there may be food in My house, and try Me now in this," says the Lord of hosts, "If I will not open for you the windows of heaven and pour out for you such blessing that there will not be room enough to receive it."
>
> Malachi 3:10

I began tithing at a difficult time in my life, right after a divorce. I had very little money, facing unemployment or relocation with the company to a place where my son and I didn't know a soul. A Christian friend advised that I couldn't afford not to tithe, and I figured that I had nothing to lose. I was a new Christian at that time; however, I tithed one-tenth of my before-tax income and sponsored an orphan through an international organization, even though I had to eat supermarket microwave lunch for a while. God works in mysterious ways. Even today, I still can't comprehend how He paid the divorce attorney fee, moved us out of the house and into a townhouse, got me a job in Atlanta, and made sure my son and I were never short of material things. In fact, people accuse me of having too many clothes and jewelry; I have to give some away to make room for more that come my way. But the blessing of knowing that the Creator of the Universe is working in my life has much exceeded the material increase. God came into my life as my Savior at the appointed time to pull me out of the pit. I couldn't handle divorce; I had never imagined that it would happen to me and force me to raise a child all by myself in a foreign land.

I don't limit tithe and giving to 10%. A few years ago, on the New Year's Day when I fasted and prayed for direction of the coming year, God instructed me to tithe 15%. I prayed several more times wishing I had heard God wrong, but He insisted on 15%. I reviewed my budget; the only thing that could go was my personal expenses. I mentioned to a choir friend that I couldn't go shopping anymore. It was during that year that God filled my closet with all kinds of clothes, and I didn't even have enough room for them. God blessed me with what I was willing to give up to obey and a chance to learn a good lesson of faith.

Besides giving to the churches, Christian workers, and ministries, we also need to take care of our families and give to the poor. "But if anyone does not provide for his own, and especially for those of his household, he has denied the faith and is worse than an unbeliever" (1 Timothy 5:8). The husband should provide for his wife and children; the wife should bring income or profit to benefit the home. Parents should take care of their children, helping them to get a good education and become financially independent. When aging parents can't take care of themselves anymore, grown children should assume responsibilities for their financial, health, and emotional needs. The Proverbs 31 woman worked hard to provide for her family. "She also rises while it is yet night, and provides food for her household, and a portion for her maidservants" (Proverbs 31:15). She also bought real estate, and from the profit she planted a vineyard

(Proverbs 31:16). She made nice, warm clothes for her families and sold linen garments and sashes (Proverbs 31:21–22, 24). This virtuous woman did not waste any time in idleness; she understood her responsibilities as a wife and mother. Because of her diligence, her husband could devote his time to do his work knowing that she was trustworthy. Her children appreciated her loving tender care and called her blessed, and her husband also praised her (Proverbs 31:28).

Three months before my mother went to the Lord, I went home to spend two weeks of Christmas vacation with her. I didn't know that it would be my last visit with her in Taiwan. The Saturday morning after returning from the long trip, when I was on my knees thanking God for the time I had with my mother, God revealed to me that He was going to take her very soon. I was learning to hear from God at that time and was devastated with the message; however, it was crystal clear. I rushed to the phone to call Mother; she was well. I then went to her favorite clothing store to get her a birthday gift. I shared with a Christian friend what God had disclosed, and she said that it was to ease my pain when it actually happened. I was on guard for a while and then decided not to be bothered; after all, I might have not heard from God. I called Mother on her birthday in February, and she was happy with the gift, even though she said I shouldn't have spent more money on her after all the gifts I had brought to her in December. She complained about stomach pain, but I didn't relate that to what God had said to me in early January. The day before my birthday in early March, my sister called to say our mother had been diagnosed with liver cancer, and there was nothing the doctors could do. I took family leave from work without pay, not knowing what to expect when I returned; the intent was to stay in Taiwan to care for Mother for as long as it was necessary.

Besides the nurse, among my sister, brothers, and I, one of us stayed with Mother in the hospital at night. One night, my sister was supposed to stay with Mother, but she asked me if I would stay instead. She was bothered that Mother coughed blood out of her mouth during the day. I was pretty shaken up as well; however, when I looked at my sister, I knew that she needed a break. Shortly after midnight, Mother suddenly woke up in severe pain; both the nurse and the doctor came to help her. They tried all they could, but nothing worked. "Mom, Jesus Christ is the only person who can help you. Ask Him to save you," I cried desperately. In agony she asked Jesus Christ to save her, and her pain subsided miraculously within a few minutes. She then asked Jesus Christ to take her home voluntarily. She went back to sleep peacefully, and I was in awe with what had happened. I had prayed for Mother's salvation for a long time, and suddenly God had showed up at His appointed time to make His move. God had mercy on me because He made sure I was there to hold her hands.

The next day at about the same time, the doctor informed me that it could be that night or in the next few days that Mother would pass away. I called to wake up my siblings, they all came to Mother, and we decided that we would all stay with her day and night until her last minute. A few hours later, we watched her heart rate go down to zero. I put Mother's birthday gift on her; she went to the Lord looking pretty, wearing the dress I bought her. Death is a miracle, just like birth, and God is in total control.

I cleaned up Mother's house after the funeral, keeping my youngest brother, whom she lived with after Father deceased, company for a while, and then took a two-week trip around the New York area with all my siblings. We assessed what we still had after both parents had passed away. The first Mother's Day without Mother, the five of us were together, cruising New York City. "Today is Mother's Day," my sister whispered sadly. I looked at her compassionately and replied, "She is in heaven now." Tears came down on my face. I will always miss her. I respected her faithfulness to my father, her love for all her children, her kindness toward people, and her fun-loving attitude for life. It took me a while to recover from not getting paid for three months and making the trips, but it was worth it. When I think of Mother now, I know that I did the best I could to care for her during her last days on earth, and God answered my prayers for her salvation.

In Matthew 25:40, Jesus Christ identified Himself with the poor, "…'Assuredly, I say to you, inasmuch as you did it to one of the least of these My brethren, you did it to Me.'" The Proverbs 31 woman had set a good example for us: "She extends her hand to the poor, yes, she reaches out her hands to the needy" (Proverbs 31:20). One Friday morning when I tuned into Meyer's *Enjoying Everyday Life*, the program before hers, *Outreach International*, was asking for donations to provide water for the people in remote countries. God instructed me to make a donation. I called and heard my voice shaking; the images of the poor children on TV were in my mind. I was grateful that God used me to provide water for some of them. They need water, something we take for granted everyday. It was a small donation; however, nothing God tells me to do is too small.

I should also give to encourage the blessed. A good friend was getting married, and I was happy that God brought her a mate. I prayed, and God said to give her a nice nightgown. God once told me to bless two of my best friends from high school with a pair of earrings and a book. Everybody needs encouragement, and a gift says, "I am thinking about you." When we love someone, we need to put love into action. God instructed me to give Meyer a pair of earrings that I had had for twenty-five years, which I bought in Taiwan shortly before I moved to the United States. I consider it my privilege to give Meyer something that is close to my heart; Mother helped me pick them out before I left home for graduate school at Auburn University, which turned into a lifelong journey. One Saturday evening when I watched Stanley on TV, I asked God what I could do to bless him; God said to send him a tie.

I am blessed with an earthly father who taught me to give back to the communities. My father was a businessman; he provided for his family well. Even though he didn't have a lot of money, he was rich in many ways. Family was his priority; he loved my mother and cared for all his children. He polished my shoes for me every evening until I left home for college. When I think of my father, the most precious memory was that he often took me along when he played golf. These were the father and daughter special times, when I always got a treat of my favorite iced tea, the kind that had condensed milk in it, and a fancy lunch with him at the club. When I was growing up, he believed in discipline, discipline, and discipline. Family dinner was mandatory; over the dinner table, he taught us about family values, integrity, and giving back to the communities. He did a lot of volunteer work with the police department to secure the neighborhood and helped found a business school in my hometown. Hundreds of people from the communities, as well as many teachers and students from the business school, came to his funeral to pay him respect.

When a Christian tithes due to love and obedience to the heavenly Father, it is an act of worship. I don't tithe to get something out of God or to impress other people. If I don't tithe properly, I rob God.

> Will a man rob God? Yet you have robbed Me!
> But you say, "In what way have we robbed You?"
> In tithes and offerings. You are cursed with a curse,
> for you have robbed Me, even this whole nation.
>
> Malachi 3:8–9

I give with a cheerful attitude and don't expect return from the recipients. It is a gift, not a deal. When I tithe and give according to God's will, I can anticipate material increase. The increase doesn't come from the ministries or the people I give to; it comes from God in His timing and creative ways. God is generous and gracious; I can't give more than Him. He has blessed me with everything I need, including the things I don't know I need.

> ... For all that is in heaven and in earth is Yours; Yours is the kingdom, O Lord, and You are exalted as head over all. Both riches and honor come from You, and You reign over all. In Your hand is power and might; in Your hand it is to make great and to give strength to all.
>
> 1 Chronicles 29:11–12

God owns everything in the heavens and earth; He is the Master and I am the steward, a manager of His possessions. God decides what He gives to me, and I am to be content and faithful with all that He has entrusted me. I count my blessings every day.

Fellowship with Other Christians

> Two are better than one, because they have a good reward for their labor. For if they fall, one will lift up his companion. But woe to him who is alone when he falls, for he has no one to help him up.
>
> Ecclesiastes 4:9–10

God works through people. I pray for God to bring me Christian friends and trust His divine connections. Only God knows people's hearts, which are more important than appearance. I go extra miles for the people whom God puts on my path to love. They may come into my life for a reason, for a season, or for a lifetime; however, they all make an impact on my Christian walk. Each time I obey God's leading into a relationship, it enriches my life.

Involvement with people is delicate. It requires maturity to become involved and not to be influenced negatively. The most common problem in relationship today is moving into depth too quickly; the drive-thru relationship is only situational and doesn't last long. Women have more problems in this area than men; they look for love in the wrong places. A relationship can't fix their problems; only God can fill the void in each person's life. In *TODAY MATTERS*, John Maxwell urged people not to seek relationships for their own gain.

> To make sure your motives are right, take this advice from Leo Buscaglia, who wrote *Loving Each Other*: "Always start a relationship by asking: Do I have ulterior motives for wanting to relate to this person? Is my caring conditional? Am I trying to escape something? Am I planning to change the person? Do I need this person to help me make up for a deficiency in myself? If your answer to any of these questions is 'yes,' leave the person alone. He or she is better off without you."[4]

We should seek divine connections to add value to people's lives. On the other hand, God instructs us to choose our friends carefully (Proverbs 12:26). Examine the lives of your close friends to see if they are living in God's will. Do not seek counsel of people who do not obey God.

Jesus Christ had many acquaintances; like Jesus Christ, we need to interact with fellow Christians and non-believers. We should be kind to people but not allow them to control us.

> For though I am free from all men, I have made myself a servant to all, that I might win the more; and to the Jews I became as a Jew, that I might win Jews; to those who are under the law, as under the law, that I might win those who are under the law; to those who are without law, as without law (not being without law toward God, but under law toward Christ), that I might win those who are without law; to the weak I became as weak, that I might win the weak. I have become all things to all men, that I might by all means save some.
>
> 1 Corinthians 9:19–22

Paul didn't allow people to control him or compromise godly principles, but he was flexible to adapt his approach to different groups of people. If I am to witness to vegetarians, I can give up eating meat, but I won't participate in gossip. Meyer said that we need to be sensitive to other people's situations. When someone shares how he or she suffers from sickness, it is not the time to share our instant healing. God commands His children to love their brothers. "My little children, let us not love in word or in tongue, but in deed and in truth" (1 John 3:18). In today's society, let's begin with words. Love is not rude. Some people don't say "Hi," or "How are you?" to greet people; instead they say something nasty, insulting, or even twist the truth to get attention. Manipulation is not communication. It is sad to hear this kind of conversation at church; Solomon knew how to handle them. "Better to dwell in a corner of a house-top, than in a house shared with a contentious woman" (Proverbs 21:9). The Psalm writer marveled at Jesus Christ's gracious speech (Psalm 45:2); when we speak, we should imitate Jesus Christ. John Maxwell remarked in *TODAY MATTERS*,

> I believe every human being deserves to be treated with respect because everyone has value. I also have observed that giving people respect first is one of the most *effective* ways of interacting with others. However, that doesn't mean you can demand respect in return. You must earn it. If you respect yourself, respect others, and exhibit competence, others will almost always give you respect. If everyone treated others with respect, the world would be a better place.[5]

After Jesus Christ went to a mountain to pray all night, He chose twelve apostles. Nine of them were his companions but not His most intimate friends. Jesus Christ only took Peter, James, and John to the Mount of Transfiguration. Only those three were asked to watch with Him at Gethsemane. We need to set limits like Jesus Christ. Christian love doesn't mean I become everyone's intimate friend, which is technically impossible; however, I should treat all people with love and respect. To choose an intimate friend, you should first examine your friend's relationship with God. A person who loves God will be faithful to his friends. You should also select a friend who has integrity. I prefer to be with people who encourage me instead of those who put me down. I stay away from people who complain or gossip too much. Trustworthy and faithful friends are scarce, and even divine connections take time to mature. Real friends remain faithful no matter what happens in our lives. They are the people who call to check on me and take me to lunch when I don't have a job. They tell about my strengths in public and correct me in private, and I can trust them to keep my private things private. They bring out the best in me, and I bring out the best in them. More people will help me when I am in tight places, but only real friends will be happy when I succeed. For example, God instructed me to write devotional e-mails; I was amazed with how many people God touched by them. However, I found out that I didn't have any real friends. No one was happy that God used me to accomplish His purpose. I was envied, slandered, and insulted by my *friends*. But there is a friend who will never leave me or forsake me; His name is Jesus Christ. He comforted me when I lost faith in people and brought me new friends.

I forgot where I read this story of a goldfish, and if I have changed something about it, it now goes like this: "When I was growing up, one day my goldfish died. I cried for three days and then buried it in the backyard. I went to the aquarium to find myself a bigger and better goldfish, and life went on." Meyer said that when she answered God's call to preach, she lost all her friends. They told her that she couldn't make it because she was a woman and didn't have the *right* personality. My old friends declared that I was a foreigner and not supposed to be more blessed than them or used by God. I am determined to go with God wherever He leads, and life goes on. I have buried the past in my backyard; it is time for a new beginning. He will bring me fellow Christians in His timing, with whom I can be free as a foreigner and be blessed; together we can make a difference in God's kingdom.

Proceed with each relationship slowly; give it time to build a solid foundation. In each relationship, you can expect problems. Pray for God's wisdom to see the problems in His perspective. Be ready to forgive immediately. I sometimes struggle with forgiveness when people insult me in public. God showed me 1 Peter 2:15: "For this is the will of God, that by doing good you may put to silence the ignorance of foolish men." God's way is for me to keep quiet and continue to do the good works He has called me to do. I shouldn't be concerned with what others have done to me; I should only be concerned with how I treat them.

> To speak evil of no one, to be peaceable, gentle, showing all humility to all men. For we ourselves were also once foolish, disobedient, deceived, serving various lusts and pleasures, living in malice and envy, hateful and hating one another.
>
> Titus 3:2–3

True humility is not to think about myself but to obey God in all things. I should forgive, overcome evil with good, and pray for people who persecuted me, for they didn't know that they were used by the devil to make me quit God's callings. I should focus on God's purposes in my life. I no longer exist; Jesus Christ lives His life through me. I shouldn't be distracted by the baits of the devil. But in extreme physical or verbal abuse, I don't have to stay in that situation. Jesus Christ walked away when people tried to stone Him. David turned from his brother (1 Samuel 17:30); he didn't have time to deal with his brother's pettiness. David might not have been the people's choice of king; however, he was God's choice and knew who he was in Christ. In the situation that people try to tempt me into sin, I shall run; I wish Eve had run instead of allowing the devil to talk to her. I can still pray, forgive people in my heart, and leave judgment in God's hands.

When you finally find the people who can be your intimate friends, be sure not to take them for granted. That's when relationships fade. Loyal friends are hard to find, and good relationships require a lot of effort. Encourage them to reach their full potential, and celebrate their successes. It is very important to give your friends the space they need. If we spend too much time together, we may outwear our welcome. Be sensitive to their needs and love them unconditionally.

> For I know that in me (that is, in my flesh) nothing good dwells; for to will is present with me, but how to perform what is good I do not find. For the good that I will to do, I do not do; but the evil I will not to do, that I practice. Now if I do what I will not to do, it is no longer I who do it, but sin that dwells in me.
>
> Romans 7:18–20

Paul knew that we don't have control of ourselves; it is only by giving our lives to Jesus Christ that we can come under the control of the Holy Spirit to leave our sinful nature. In Spirit-Controlled Temperament, Tim LaHaye cited,

> There is nothing more fascinating about people than their inherited temperament! ... Temperament provides both our strengths and weaknesses. Although we like to think only of our strengths, everyone has weaknesses! ... Temperament traits, whether controlled or uncontrolled, last throughout life ... The Holy Spirit can, however, modify our temperaments so that they appear to have been changed.[6]

He also remarked that most people are a blend of two or more of those temperament types: Sanguine, Choleric, Melancholy, and Phlegmatic.[7] Understanding temperaments helps me to accept others and myself and to improve relationships among intimate friends and acquaintances. God created man in His own image. The psalmist praised God for His creation. "I will praise You, for I am fearfully and wonderfully made; marvelous are Your works, and that my soul knows very well" (Psalm 139:14). God saw that all He made was good, but sin snaked into the world. We all need the Holy Spirit to guide and correct in order to be more like Jesus Christ.

Sanguine temperaments are charming, friendly, compassionate, spontaneous, creative, and emotional people. They are outgoing talkers who love to have fun. They like people so much that when they give you their five minutes' attention, make sure you know that it is not affection. They make you feel like you are their best friend. However, someone else will get their attention five minutes later. Don't be surprised if they don't remember your name next week. Sanguines talk easily with strangers; they never lack instant friends. But they are disorganized, inconsistent, restless, undisciplined, unproductive, unstable, may not finish tasks, may not tell the truth, and do not learn from past mistakes.

Apostle Peter is my favorite Sanguine in the Bible. He left his fishing business to follow Jesus Christ spontaneously; I wonder if his wife made any comments about that. Peter, the talker, always had the wrong thing to say at the right time. Out of his compassion for Jesus Christ, he told Jesus Christ that crucifixion should never have happened to Him (Matthew 16:22). Peter should have listened to Jesus Christ instead of talking and expressing his own ideas. When Jesus Christ showed up at night, walking on the sea, the disciples were terrified. Jesus Christ said to them: "Be of good cheer! It is I; do not be afraid." Peter was the only person who got out of the boat and walked on the water toward Jesus Christ. When he took his eyes off Jesus Christ, he began to sink (Matthew 14:25–30). Sanguines talk and act without plan; they make decisions out of emotion. But we should give Peter credit for getting out of the boat while everyone else stayed put. To answer God's calling, get out of your boat! You may sink, but Jesus Christ will be there to catch you.

Peter's night fishing trip on the Sea of Galilee was a failure. But when Jesus Christ said to him, "Launch out into the deep and let down your nets for a catch," (Luke 5:4) he replied, "Master, we have toiled all night and caught nothing; nevertheless at Your word I will let down the net" (Luke5:5). They caught such a large number of fish that they signaled their partners in the other boat to come and help; two boats began to sink with the catch (Luke 5:7). When we obey God without reasoning, we experience God's presence and mighty power; we also bring blessings to other people. God uses Peter's fishing story to encourage me to obey with complete trust. "Trust in the Lord with all your heart, and lean not on your own understanding; in all your ways acknowledge Him, and He shall direct your paths" (Proverbs 3:5).

Eleanor Lewis commented in *How to Accept Yourself, Understand Others, and Like them Anyway!!!* that Sanguines often have good intentions but may lack discipline or self-control to follow through with them. "Peter said to Him, 'Even if I have to die with You, I will not deny You!'" (Matthew 26:35). But he denied Jesus Christ three times, just like Jesus Christ prophesied. I take Peter's failure to heart; I pray for God to give me strength so that I don't deny Him. When we are tired, weak, and weary, denying Jesus Christ can happen to all of us in a subtle way. In spite of his weaknesses and failures, God used Peter, the talker, to preach the Gospels after resurrection. God gave Peter the key of the kingdom, and he used it to open the doors of faith for the Jews, the Samaritans, and the Gentiles. Sanguines need self-control; after the Holy Spirit came at Pentecost, when Peter addressed the crowd, he was filled with the Holy Spirit. After God filled the disciples with the Holy Spirit, they didn't argue among themselves about who was God's favorite disciple anymore; they were busy doing God's work.

Cholerics are confident, competitive, independent, productive, organized, goal-oriented, decisive, practical, strong-willed, and unemotional people. They are doers who can't sit still. They were born to rule the world. Because they are so insensitive, impatient, opinionated, self-sufficient, and unforgiving, they don't have good relationships with people. Choleric is my first temperament; I didn't know how to love people until God came into my life. I still struggle with impatience and unforgiveness.

Paul is my favorite Choleric in the Bible. He liked to work so much that he wrote Romans, 1 Corinthians, 2 Corinthians, Galatians, Ephesians, Philippians, Colossians, 1 Thessalonians, 2 Thessalonians, 1 Timothy, 2 Timothy, Titus, Philemon, and Hebrews. Without Paul, we wouldn't have as much to study in the New Testament. Cholerics take a stand. Before Paul was converted, he was busy persecuting Christians, who he thought were evil. After Paul met Jesus Christ on his way to Damascus, he took a stand for Jesus Christ even unto death. Cholerics are born leaders who don't need to have authority to lead and to influence. When Paul was a prisoner sailing to Rome, he was in charge during the storm. Cholerics like to be in control; they make good and instant decisions.

Cholerics are determined people, they don't give up easily, and adversity doesn't frighten them. I believe that there are some things I can only learn from trials. In the midst of the storms, I should mount up with wings like eagles and stay above the circumstances. Paul endured many hardships, and he remained faithful to God's callings. "Serving the Lord with all humility, with many tears and trials which happened to me by the plotting of the Jews" (Acts 20:19). He served God with tears; however, he said, "I have fought the good fight, I have finished the race, I have kept the faith" (2 Timothy 4:7). In spite of numerous storms and dangers, Paul moved the Gospels from the Jews to the Gentiles and from Jerusalem to Rome.

Cholerics don't sympathize easily with others. They tend to be goal-oriented; they are not sensitive to other people's feelings. They will get rid of the people who stand in their way to accomplish what they set out to do. They are bored with details. When you push Cholerics, they will push back. All of these traits lead to poor relationships. However, they can certainly cut through the crap to get things done. If they have to, they will kick the door open and take over.

> Now Barnabas was determined to take with them John called Mark. But Paul insisted that they should not take with them the one who had departed from them in Pamphylia, and had not gone with them to the work. Then the contention became so sharp that they parted from one another …
>
> Acts 15:37–39

Paul wasn't ready to forgive Mark then; instead he enlisted Timothy to take Mark's place. He did eventually forgive Mark and accepted him again. It is very hard for Cholerics to forgive; we can only do it under the influence of the Holy Spirit. Wiersbe remarked, "If God had to depend on perfect people to accomplish His work, He would never ever get anything done. Our limitations and imperfections are good reasons for us to depend on the grace of God, for our sufficiency is from Him alone (2 Cor. 3:5)."[8]

Melancholies are analytical, accurate, dependable, thoughtful, detailed, faithful, gifted, self-sacrificing, and sensitive perfectionists. They are deep thinkers who don't need to talk. They need to collect much information to analyze before they make a decision; they want to do it right. They tend to be too serious, unsociable, easily offended, depressed, negative, insecure, critical, and suspicious. Because of their perfectionism, they don't make friends easily; however, when they finally do, they are usually the most faithful friends for life.

My favorite Melancholy in the Bible is Moses. Moses wrote Genesis, Exodus, Leviticus, Numbers, and Deuteronomy in the Old Testament. This gifted perfectionist did whatever he did well. But Melancholies are usually distressed with the imperfection in people and circumstances. Even though they are extremely gifted and talented, they are insecure and lack self-confidence. God appeared to Moses in a burning bush and asked Moses to deliver Israel, but he thought God made a mistake in choosing him.

> "Come now, therefore, and I will send you to Pharaoh that you may bring My people, the children of Israel, out of Egypt." But Moses said

to God, "Who am I that I should go to Pharaoh, and that I should bring the children of Israel out of Egypt?" So He said, "I will certainly be with you…"

Exodus 3:10–12

Moses had no confidence in himself, and even after God promised to be with him, he was still fearful and suspicious. He then questioned God's identity, which reminded me of the grocery store line conversation: "God, May I see your driver's license, please?" God said to Moses that He was the great I AM, the God of his fathers, the God of Abraham, the God of Isaac, and the God of Jacob (Exodus 3:14–15). "Then Moses answered and said, 'But suppose they will not believe me or listen to my voice; suppose they say, 'The Lord has not appeared to you'" (Exodus 4:1). God then conducted two miracles to convince Moses. Moses analyzed the situation and told God that he had never been eloquent and that he was slow of speech and slow of tongue (Exodus 4:10). "'Now therefore, go, and I will be with your mouth and teach you what you shall say.' But, He said, 'O my Lord, please send by the hand of whomever else you may send'" (Exodus 4:12–13). I can feel my own impatience. I would have been jumping up and down, shouting, "Thank you, Lord, for choosing me." Why in the world would he miss the chance of a lifetime? I may sink once in a while, but Jesus Christ will be there to catch me.

Moses was faithful to carry on his calling until he dishonored God by disobeying God's instruction. God told Moses to speak to the rock, and it would pour out water to provide for the community. However, Moses was mad at people, and instead he struck the rock twice with his staff. The consequence was that Moses didn't enter the Promised Land. God loved Moses so much that when Moses died, God buried his body Himself; no one knew where Moses' grave was. Melancholy is the richest and most gifted temperament; many important Bible characters were strong Melancholies, like Moses, Elijah, Solomon, and Apostle John. They don't have to strive to be faithful; they are faithful by nature.

I work in the IT (Information Technology) industry and have been trained to look for problems. But when it comes to people, I can't be so critical; I need to forgive and give mercy. God has showed me that I shouldn't depend on my analysis to make decisions; I should obey the Holy Spirit's prompting moment by moment in confidence. Melancholies have the tendency to be fearful. "For God has not given us a spirit of fear, but of power and of love and of a sound mind." (2 Timothy 1:7) is one of the Bible verses that I have memorized.

Phlegmatics are patient, kind, easy-going, laid back, dependable, diplomatic, persistent, efficient, and capable people. They are watchers who are not very much involved and look for the easy way out. They don't lack of friends because they enjoy people and are naturally nice. They are usually calm, cool, and sympathetic, but they tend to be indecisive, unenthusiastic, procrastinating, selfish, unmotivated, stubborn, and not aggressive. When they finally put their acts together and get to work, they are actually very capable and efficient.

Abraham is my favorite Phlegmatic in the Bible. When Abraham was seventy-five years old, God said to him, "Get out of your country, from your family and from your father's house, to a land that I will show you" (Genesis 12:1). Phlegmatics are family people; instead of leaving his father's household, Abraham took his father and nephew with him. His father, Terah, delayed the journey, and Abraham stayed in Haran until Terah died before he went to Canaan. At Bethel there was quarreling between Abram's and Lot's herdsmen because the land they stayed on couldn't support both of them. The kind and easy-going Abraham let Lot choose for himself the whole plain of the Jordan, and Lot set out toward the east.

> And the Lord said to Abram, after Lot had separated from him: "Lift your eyes now and look from the place where you are—northward, southward, eastward and westward; for all the land which you see I give to you and your descendants forever."
>
> Genesis 13:14–15

Due to fear and self-protection, Abraham partially obeyed God by taking along his father and nephew on the journey; however, "There is no wisdom or understanding or counsel against the Lord" (Proverbs 21:30). God has a way to get His will done the way He wants it done.

God promised Abraham and Sarah lots of descendants. "Then He brought him outside and said, 'Look now toward heaven, and count the stars if you are able to number them.' and He said to him, 'So shall your descendants be'" (Genesis 15:5). They waited many years and still had no children; Sarah took the matter into her own hands. She gave her Egyptian maidservant Hagar to Abraham to be his wife so that she could build a family through Hagar. Abraham did what she said to avoid conflict; Phlegmatics desire peace at all times and avoid conflicts as much as possible. Hagar bore him a son, Ishmael, and that was the beginning of strife. Sarah did become pregnant and bore a son, Isaac, to Abraham in his old age at the appointed time as God had promised him. Ishmael became the forefather of the Arabs, and the God given son Isaac was the forefather of the Jews. If only Abraham and Sarah would have waited for God to bring His promises to pass, the earth would have been a better place to live.

When I think of Abraham, I think of faith. In spite of his temperament weaknesses, he was faithful to God, even willing to sacrifice the son, whom he waited twenty plus years for. God tested Abraham's faithfulness:

> Then He said, "Take now your son, your only son Isaac, whom you love, and go to the land of Moriah, and offer him there as a burnt offering on one of the mountains of which I shall tell you."
>
> Genesis 22:2

Abraham did what God told him to do, and when he reached out his hand to take the knife to slay his son, the angel of the Lord called out to him from heaven. "And He said, 'Do not lay your hand on the lad, or do anything to him; for now I know that you fear God, since you have not withheld your son, your only son, from Me'" (Genesis 22:12). What a faithful man; he trusted God with the consequences. Has your faith ever been tested by God? My most recent experience was unemployment, and God used this time to let me finish the manuscript of this book, which I started three years ago. I have found my answer in Psalm 66:10–12:

> For You, O God, have tested us; You have refined us as silver is refined. You brought us into the net; You laid affliction on our backs. You have caused men to ride over our heads; We went through fire and through water; but You brought us out to rich fulfillment."
>
> Psalm 66:10–12

Phlegmatics tend to be spectators in life and don't get too much involved with the activities of others. They need to move as soon as they hear from God instead of waiting until God puts a fire underneath them to get them going. Phlegmatic is my least favorite temperament. I dislike people who don't have the courage to take a stand for what they believe, but God surrounds me with them. God doesn't give me what I want; He gives me what I need. I need the strengths of the Phlegmatics to complement my weaknesses. I have finally learned to wait for God's timing instead of getting ahead of Him. I have watched the slow Phlegmatics stay calm and cool when I stressed myself out. They still get to my nerves when they take too long, but I have realized that if God doesn't move, nothing is going to get done. It is God who is in control. I shouldn't strive, just abide.

Sanguines and Cholerics are outgoing people. They strive on activities; just watching them, you will get tired. If Peter and Paul went fishing together, Peter would have been telling fish stories while Paul caught many fish. The other two temperaments, Melancholy and Phlegmatic, are the introverts. During the fishing trip, the Melancholy would be sitting in the back of the boat studying how to fish before he did it; the Phlegmatic would be lying next to him doing nothing. Understanding temperaments doesn't mean I will never get frustrated; however, it helps me to know why people behave certain ways and learn to appreciate the differences. God puts people on my path for me to love and to enjoy, not to make over. Creation is done; I can't change people. Each person is God's masterpiece; I need to look for the good instead of the imperfection. God uses imperfect people to accomplish His perfect plan.

Evangelize

"And He said to them, 'Go into all the world and preach the gospel to every creature'" (Mark 16:15). If you have believed in Jesus Christ and enjoyed His grace, mercy, and blessings, share the good news of salvation with others that they may have eternal life. This is the ultimate calling of all Christians. The evangelists were God's gift to the early churches (Ephesians 4:11); they traveled from place to place to preach the Gospels to whom the Holy Spirit led them. The early disciples were also called evangelists (Acts 8:4) because they went everywhere preaching the Word. All Christians today should continue witnessing like the early evangelists; speak and write of Jesus Christ and bring the good news of eternal life to the lost.

How do we bring the good news of the Gospels to the lost? Apostle Paul demonstrated this in 1 Corinthians 2:3–5:

> I was with you in weakness, in fear, and in much trembling. And my speech and my preaching were not with persuasive words of human wisdom, but in demonstration of the Spirit and of power, that your faith should not be in the wisdom of men but in the power of God.
>
> 1 Corinthians 2:3–5

He didn't depend on his own strengths but simply declared God's Word. He knew that his letters would grieve those he loved, and he wrote with tears and sorrow in his heart. He could have exercised his authority and commanded people to obey him, but he chose to minister with patience, humility, and love (2 Corinthians 2:2–3). We should evangelize with a compassionate heart without compromising the truth. "Behold, I send you out as sheep in the midst of wolves. Therefore be wise as serpents and harmless as doves" (Matthew 10:16). When the Holy Spirit leads you, evangelize anywhere and anytime. Let your faith shine through, be the salt and the light wherever God puts you, and be a blessing. Stanley's Life Principle 25 says, "God blesses us so that we might bless others."[9]

Evangelism starts with our families. Families are the most difficult people to convert; we don't do well in our hometown. It will take a lot of prayers, patience, and love to preach to our families. I pray daily for my family's salvation. God saved my parents, my oldest brother, my son, and me; He will have mercy for the rest of my family if they will also believe.

While Paul and Silas were praying and singing hymns to God in Philippi prison, God sent a great earthquake. The foundations of the prison were shaken, and immediately all the doors were opened and everyone's chains loosed. The keeper of the prison thought that the prisoners had fled. He was about to kill himself when Paul said in a loud voice, "Do yourself no harm, for we are all here." The jailer brought them out and said, "Sirs, what must I do to be saved?" So they said, "Believe on the Lord Jesus Christ, and you will be saved, you and your household" (Acts 16:25–31). This did not mean that the jailer's family would be automatically saved; his household would be saved if they would also believe. Wiersbe commented, "So-called 'household salvation' has no basis in the Word of God—that is, that the decision of the head of the household brings salvation to the members of the household."[10] Each one of us must trust Jesus Christ personally to receive salvation. My family is the most precious group of people in my life, and they are worthy of my time and effort to share God's Word when the Holy Spirit leads me. Unless God is at work, there can be no salvation.

When we go to work, church, and the communities, we enter the mission fields. The Proverbs 31 woman was excellent, and her life was a testimony to others; other people in the community praised her (Proverbs 31:29,31). God calls me to work in the market place, and that's my mission field. I can't preach the Gospels freely at work, but I can be an excellent employee to glorify God. "And whatever you do, do it heartily, as to the Lord and not to men, knowing that from the Lord you will receive the reward of the inheritance; for you serve the Lord Christ" (Colossians 3:23–24). Even when my boss is not fair to me, I show him respect. Though my contribution is not being recognized, I serve God with skills and great attitude. In every relationship, we can expect problems. This is when Christians behave differently from the non-believers. The Bible teaches us how to handle relationships. King Saul wanted to kill David due to his jealousy. David had two chances to kill Saul, but He trusted God to handle His anointed King. David didn't kill to take his throne; he waited for God to put him there. David demonstrated how we should treat our authorities, regardless of how they treat us. I don't bad mouth my co-workers to get ahead; I go extra miles for my customers to help them achieve their goals. I may be the only Bible people at work read. God is in control of what I do; I serve God with excellence to glorify Him. I can't stay at the same place forever to serve God; when God moves, I follow. God always has a purpose for each job He places me in. A job is a call for service.

Have you ever been stressed out by your job? I have been there a few times when I strived with effort and worked for the wrong people: men instead of God. It is very tiring to please people because it is impossible. I need to respect human authorities but ask the Holy Spirit to guide me on how and when to do my assignments. When I depend on my own strengths and judgment and try to meet people's unrealistic expectation, I am out of God's will.

Abide instead of strive. "I am the vine, you are the branches. He who abides in Me, and I in him, bears much fruits; for without Me you can do nothing" (John

15:5). Wiersbe remarked, "What does it mean to 'abide'? It means to keep in fellowship with Christ so that His life can work in and through us to produce fruit."[11] He also commented that we will experience the Father's pruning so that we will bear more fruit. "This abiding relationship is natural to the branch and the vine, but it must be cultivated in the Christian life. It is not automatic. Abiding in Christ demands worship, meditation on God's Word, prayer, sacrifice and service ..."[12] My self-effort at work does not take me very far. I need to abide and let Jesus Christ live His life through me to produce fruit.

Make sure you go to the church God wants you to go to. Don't leave a church because it has problems; leave only when God leads you. We can't follow people. We need to obey God and completely surrender where we worship and serve. Apostle Paul pointed out to the Corinthians that they were guilty of glorying men.

> Therefore let no one boast in men. For all things are yours: whether Paul or Apollos or Cephas, or the world or life or death, or things present or things to come—all are yours. And you are Christ's, and Christ is God's.
>
> 1 Corinthians 3:21–23

If we glory men, even godly men like Peter, Paul, and Apollos, we are robbing God of the glory that He alone deserves. It was this sinful attitude of pride that was helping to cause division in the church (Wiersbe).[13]

If churchgoers and church staff don't obey God's Word and completely surrender their lives to Him, they may not have a relationship with God. Some of the churchgoers don't behave better than the non-believers; they belittle, lie, covet, make false accusations, gossip, and slander God's people. It doesn't matter how much Bible knowledge they have; knowledge without love destroys. Examine their spiritual fruits. Just listen to what people say, which comes out from their hearts, and you can tell their spiritual maturity. The carnal men are the babes in Christ (1 Corinthians 3:1). "for you are still carnal. For where there are envy, strife, and divisions among you, are you not carnal and behaving like mere men?" (1 Corinthians 3:3). Live a godly life in front of them and pray for the people who have hurt you. "If it is possible, as much as depends on you, live peaceably with all men" (Romans 12:18). But we can't seek peace at all costs; we can't compromise God's truth. In his book *THE BAIT OF SATAN*, Dr. John Revere said

> A peacemaker will confront in love, bringing truth so that the resulting reconciliation will endure. He will not maintain an artificial, superficial relationship. He desires openness, truth, and love. He refuses to hide offense with a political smile. He makes peace with a bold love that cannot fail.[14]

This doesn't mean that we need to confront every little offense; do not sweat the small stuff. Confront only when the Holy Spirit guides to build solid relationships to minister at church.

In January 2007, God led me to FBA. Stanley is a strong spiritual leader, and I am blessed with a pastor who preaches God's Word and doesn't compromise to please people. In July 2007, I heard an awesome testimony given by the new choir director, Rodney Brooks; he said that after he had worked at church for many years, he finally had the courage to give his life to God in front of his choir members and the entire church congregation. God's faithful servants deserve our respect and honor.

A few years ago, one Wednesday evening after choir practice, I had a discussion about mission trips with another choir member. I was struck by the thought that God had never used my Chinese heritage. I was born in Taiwan. Both my parents went to Japanese schools; my family had strong Japanese influence. The following Sunday, this choir member told me that the first China mission trip of women's ministry was on the church bulletin. I prayed, and God impressed on my heart to go. I was fearful about the political differences between China and Taiwan, but I answered God's calling. It was the first time in my life I had visited where my ancestors lived. I was the only person on the team who spoke Chinese, and God used me during the trip. What a blessing that God called me to serve Chinese people; they were the sweetest people I have ever met. They were humble and had enthusiasm to learn English and about American culture. I was amazed with how happy they were with very few material possessions. After the trip, I realized that I will always cherish my heritage, but home is where God wants me to be. I am willing to go to the end of the earth for God, and my God shall be with me. Before I went to China, I knew that I was going to suffer from the heat and humidity during summertime in that area of the world. I was sick for two weeks after I returned. But I went for God, and it was a small sacrifice for the great commission.

Each evangelist must possess the determination that Paul described in Acts 20:20–23.

> How I kept back nothing that was helpful, but proclaimed it to you, and taught you publicly and from house to house, testifying to Jews, and also to Greeks, repentance toward God and faith toward our Lord Jesus Christ. And see, now I go bound in the spirit to Jerusalem, not knowing the things that will happen to me there, except that the Holy Spirit testifies in every city, saying that chains and tribulations await me.
>
> Acts 20:20–23

In *BE ALL YOU CAN BE,* John Maxwell remarked that apostle Paul didn't have to survive; no one could stop him. Are you willing to pay the price for God?

Jesus Christ taught the great commission in Matthew 28:19–20.

> Go therefore and make disciples of all the nations, baptizing them in the name of the Father and of the Son and of the Holy Spirit, teaching them to observe all things that I have commanded you; and lo, I am with you always, even to the end of the age. Amen.
>
> Matthew 28:19–20

What Does God Require of His Followers?

What does God require of His followers? Micah 6: 8 says, "He has shown you, O man, what is good; and what does the Lord require of you but to do justly, to love mercy, and to walk humbly with your God?"

To do justly is to obey God's Word and the Holy Spirit's promptings, regardless of the circumstances. We can't act justly until we confess and repent all our sins. In Psalm 32:3–4, David described how miserable he was before he acknowledged his sin with Bathsheba to the Lord. "When I kept silent, my bones grew old through my groaning all the day long. For day and night Your hand was heavy upon me; my vitality was turned into the drought of summer." But once he confessed his sin, God forgave his iniquity and restored their fellowship. Only when our sins are forgiven by God's grace can we then live up to God's standard by following His instructions.

> I will instruct you and teach you in the way you should go; I will guide you with My eye. Do not be like the horse or like the mule, which have no understanding, which must be harnessed with bit and bridle, else they will not come near you.
>
> Psalm 32:8–9

If we don't repent from our wicked ways when God convicts us in private, He will convict us in public.

When do we obey God to act justly? Do we act justly only on Sunday mornings when we put on our church faces? We need to act justly in every area of our lives. "Therefore, whether you eat or drink, or what-

ever you do, do all to the glory of God" (1 Corinthians
10:31). Even for the small personal items like clothing,
I go shopping only when God tells me where to go.
Since I only purchase what God allows, dressing myself
is easy; I simply ask God what I should wear. Adam and
Eve sinned against God, and God started the fashion
industry. "Also for Adam and his wife the Lord God
made tunics of skin, and clothed them" (Genesis 3:21).
Our heavenly Father is the best fashion consultant; He
commands me to wear respectful clothes. However, He
has never told me to wear anything that fits the ste-
reotype of a religious person. Dressing like a refugee
coming out of the Stone Age is not a requirement of
being holy; look your best to glorify God. The Proverbs
31 woman wore fine attire, which was appropriate for
a godly woman (Proverbs 31:22). We serve a generous
God, who provides well if we humble ourselves and
obey. Two years ago, God graciously told me to drop a
few pounds, and He guided me through the weight loss
process. I have lost twenty pounds since then. Is being
overweight a sin?

Apostle Paul warned Corinthians using Old
Testament examples in 1 Corinthians 10. Even though
we are God's chosen people, we shouldn't abuse our
privileges. We shouldn't think that we can stand the
temptation of sin but need to be cautious in our con-
ducts. The Ten Commandments (Exodus 20:3–17) are
the basic responsibilities of Christians toward God, but
I often see Christians breaking the tenth commandment and not thinking that it is a sin. Wiersbe commented, "Covetous people will break all of God's com-

mandments in order to satisfy their desires, because at the heart of sin is the sin in the heart (Matt.15:19)."[15] My observation is that covetousness starts with slander; when someone starts to bad mouth about you, you know that this person is resentfully envious of you. Christians who have an intimate relationship with God are secure and content; most likely they are busy doing God's will and don't have time to be jealous of other people's callings or blessings. Action follows thinking; transformation starts with the mind. "And do not be conformed to this world, but be transformed by the renewing of your mind, that you may prove what is that good and acceptable and perfect will of God" (Romans 12:2).

To love mercy, we had to personally experience God's mercy. God so loved the world that He sent His only son to die on the cross for our sins. "Not by works of righteousness which we have done, but according to His mercy He saved us …" (Titus 3:5). We shouldn't be too critical toward the unsaved; remember how we used to behave. "For we ourselves were also once foolish, disobedient, deceived, serving various lusts and pleasures, living in malice and envy, hateful and hating one another" (Titus 3:3). After God came into my life, my family and friends knew that I had changed. How can God love me the way He does? I ask God to forgive me on a daily basis, and He loves me unconditionally.

Luke 15:11–24 is a parable of the lost son. The prodigal son asked his father to give him his portion, and he went to a far country, where he wasted all his possessions. There came a famine in that land, and he had to feed the pigs and ate pig food. He came to himself and realized that his father was a generous man and that even becoming his father's servant would be better. He repented from his sins and went back to his father; the father ran to welcome him and honored him with a feast of celebration. The father forgave his son from the heart, and we should forgive and restore people who have sinned and repented with mercy.

To walk humbly with God, we must imitate the way of the cross. Jesus Christ came to save us, not to be served. We need to obey God in all things to serve Him. It is simple but hard to walk humbly with God. It is simple because all I have to do is to obey God; it is hard because I have to deny myself, and my faith will be tested repeatedly.

There is no easy place to serve God; if it is easy, something is wrong. God's thoughts are higher than my thoughts; His will is usually not what I anticipate. To serve Him, I have to carry my cross and follow Him daily. During my early Christian days, I used to complain and argue with God; I said the worst words to God when my father died shortly after I went through divorce. But God never gave up on me; He was persistent in refining me. I used to cry out to God for His mercy to lift the pain and agony I had to endure. Just when I thought that God would change the circumstances, another trial came upon me. He pushed me beyond my limits so that I would rely solely on Him. God requires total surrender and commitment. I now embrace the storms of life, and God strengthens my faith, molds me, and redirects my life path. The result is that I have God's best for me.

Apostle Paul was ready not only to be bound but also to die in Jerusalem for the name of the Lord. He said in Acts 20:19–24 that he served the Lord with all humility, with many tears and trials. The Holy Spirit said to him that chains and tribulations awaited him. But he wasn't moved, and he wanted to finish his race with joy. David exalted our Lord even when he had to hide in the caves, and his psalms are the most quoted Scriptures in the Bible. Wiersbe wrote, "We're commanded to do everything to the glory of God (1 Cor. 10:31), and if 'everything' includes hiding in caves, then may the Lord be magnified!"[16]

Waiting is a major part of walking humbly with God. God prepares His servants before He can use them, and preparation takes a long time. Meyer said that she had cried a swimming pool of tears before God brought the vision He put on her heart to pass. Nothing can change God's plan; I might as well enjoy the ride. "For the vision is yet for an appointed time; but at the end it will speak, and it will not lie. Though it tarries, wait for it; because it will surely come, it will not tarry" (Habakkuk 2:3). God will never be late, but He will never be early. Everything happens at His appointed time. Out of God's timing is out of God's will. After Elijah had defeated the prophets of Baal, Queen Jezebel threatened to kill him for executing her false prophets, and he ran for his life. He went into a desert alone and asked God to take his life. An angel of the Lord brought him bread and water twice to strengthen him. The angel touched him and said, "Arise and eat, because the journey is too great for you." After a rest and food provided from the Lord, Elijah returned to his mission.

He traveled for another forty days and forty nights until he reached Horeb, the mountain of God. God's instructions came after the wind, the earthquake and the fire. God wasn't in the wind nor the earthquake nor the fire; He spoke in a still, small voice (1 King 19:1–13). "But those who wait on the Lord shall renew their strength; they shall mount up with wings like eagles, they shall run and not be weary, they shall walk and not faint" (Isaiah 40:31). Wait on the Lord.

What does God require of a godly woman? The Proverbs 31 woman first submitted to the Lord (Proverbs 31:30); she then submitted to her husband, and he trusted her (Proverbs 31:11). It is God's will for some people to remain single (1 Corinthians 7:8). Single women, the Lord is your husband. When a woman submits herself to the Lord, she does not have a problem submitting herself to her husband. This doesn't mean that she is less than her husband; it is the attitude that she humbles herself and allows her husband to be the head of the household, just like Jesus Christ is the head of the church. Because of the harmony in her marriage, the Proverbs 31 woman and her husband were able to raise godly children. A godly woman is first a Christian, then a wife and a mother. God is a God of order.

Live by Faith

God commanded in Habakkuk 2:4: "...But the just shall live by his faith." *Live by faith* means that we simply obey God's will in spite of feelings, circumstances, or consequences. How do we develop faith in God? "So then faith comes by hearing, and hearing by the word of God" (Romans 10:17). God said, "Let there be light," and there was light (Genesis 1:3). God spoke creation, and His Word formed all things. God spoke His promises through the Bible, and His Word will all be fulfilled in His timing. God's chosen people live on His promises, and it is *through faith and patience* that we inherit the promises (Hebrews 6:12). We should study God's Word daily and obey the Holy Spirit's prompting moment by moment with a joyful attitude.

"Thus also faith by itself, if it does not have works, is dead" (James 2:17). It is what we do in response to God's Word that speaks the level of our faith. If we don't obey God where we serve, we don't believe in God's plan and purpose for our lives, and that usually impacts other people. Jonah ran away from God's calling to preach at Nineveh. God sent a storm and threw him into the sea; a great fish that God prepared swallowed him. He repented. The Lord spoke to the fish, and it vomited Jonah onto dry land. Then Jonah went to do God's will out of fear. To his surprise, the people of Nineveh believed God; God saw that they turned from their evil ways and didn't bring disaster upon them. But Jonah was angry at God's mercy toward his repented enemies, he asked the Lord to take his life. Jonah disobeyed God and failed to look at the situation from God's perspective; his action and attitude didn't speak faith.

God is faithful; we should have faith in his faithfulness. I had a surgery a few years ago. It was my first surgery, and I didn't know how long it would take me to recover. A week later, while I was planning on going to the grocery store, a friend of mine called. When she heard what I was about to do, she said that God had told her to call, and she brought me what I needed. A few days later, I went to the grocery store by myself, and I realized that I wasn't ready until then. God provided even when I didn't know my need. He faithfully watches over all His children.

In summer of 2007, I suffered from severe allergy symptoms. I had endured allergy symptoms many years, but it was the worst that summer. I didn't believe in taking a pill every day to fix the symptoms, and most of the allergy medicine made me ill. I thought, *there must be something else that can cure me.* I prayed fervently for God's healing grace.

One day after lunch, a co-worker came to me for a ride to a bank. His car battery had malfunctioned under the extremely hot weather. I hesitated to go because I had had an upset stomach on and off for a couple of weeks, and it is unusual for me to have stomach pain. Despite my pain, I decided to help him. After we came out of the bank, my car battery didn't work either. When I went home with a new battery in the car, I felt that the summer heat had gotten to me during the ordeal.

The following week I got weaker and weaker, and finally on Friday I told my boss that I needed to rest. I then found out that my refrigerator had also stopped functioning, and it would take a few days for the new one to be delivered. I cleaned up the mess in the refrigerator and went to pick up lunch. I felt very weak to the point that I didn't feel like driving or walking. I immediately knew that God was up to something; He had allowed all these things to happen. I called a friend of mine for prayers, and she said, "Why don't you come and stay with me for a few days?" This friend was the person who introduced Jesus Christ to me when we worked for the same company about twenty years ago. She was on vacation the following week for Kenneth Copeland's Convention, and God had told her to watch the convention through the Internet from home instead of traveling. She said that she didn't know why God kept her home until I was there.

Saturday morning, we made it to the emergency room at the hospital. If my refrigerator hadn't stopped working, I would have stayed home, and it would have been a very terrifying experience to be so sick by myself. The doctor ruled out the possibility of having an infected appendix, and a week later, I went through a colonoscopy and EGD. They found bacteria in my stomach. After two weeks of heavy dosage antibiotics treatment, I was healed from stomach pain. When I stayed with my friend for a couple of days, I watched Kenneth Copeland's Convention, and God used Gloria Copeland to give me the healing Scriptures. I began to read the healing Scriptures twice a day, and God delivered me from allergy symptoms little by little as I persistently read His Word and believed that His Word had healing power. He had also provided Neti Pot (SinuCleanse® System) through my son in March 2008, nasal sprays in summer 2008, and now I believe that I am on my way to being completely free from allergy symptoms. I don't understand the path I had to go through to receive healing, but I know that God was with me through the fire. By the way, I enjoy the new bottom freezer refrigerator; it is a good gift from God with His perfect timing.

The most difficult thing that God has ever asked me to do was to let my son go live with his father after he turned into a teenager. But God had mercy on us, and my son was able to come home for a couple of weeks during summer and winter breaks while he was still in school. One summer afternoon, a couple of years after he went to California, I took him to the airport at the end of his summer visit. On my way home, I was driving toward Chattahoochee River on Roswell road. It was a three-way street with lots of trees on both sides, and the traffic in the middle lane changed directions according to the hours of the day. The rain was pouring down hard on that hot summer afternoon, and water was running on both sides of the street like roaring rivers. I had known that I needed to get new tires for my car for a long time, but I had procrastinated.

Suddenly the running water pushed my car to the middle lane, and there was a car coming from the opposite direction. The coming car was so close that I could see the terrified expression on the driver's face. A thought came into my mind, *This is it!* Right then, I expected to die. No one could survive the collision of two cars driving from opposite directions at full speed. Before I was able to react to the situation, my car moved back to the right lane by itself. You must know that I never got a chance to turn the wheels. I don't remember how I drove myself home after that incident. After I stopped crying, I got on my knees, "I give my life back to you, Lord! Use me to glorify you." I have been living my bonus days on earth since then. God is faithful in protecting His own; I have faith in Him that He will protect me, and I won't go home to Him until my work on earth is done.

The Proverbs 31 woman rejoiced in time to come (Proverbs 31:25). She was not afraid of the snow (Proverbs 31:21) or the future, because she was prepared and had faith in God that He would be with her and her family. Her relationship with God lasts through eternity.

I keep a faith journal. On the days when I am weak and double-minded, I read through the journal to remind myself of God's faithfulness and miracles that have happened to keep me on the right course with Him. "But without faith it is impossible to please Him, for he who comes to God must believe that He is, and that He is a rewarder of those who diligently seek Him" (Hebrews 11:6).

Walk in Love

God is love.

"And we have known and believed the love that God has for us. God is love, and he who abides in love abides in God, and God in him" (1 John 4:16). The Bible is a love story; it tells us how much God loves us. His love was ultimately expressed on the cross. While I was still a non-believer, God loved me first; He came into my life at the most difficult time to put me under His wings. Even when I am disappointed in myself at times, God loves me unconditionally. God loves because of who He is, not because of what I have done. It is His love that motivates me to wake up each morning and get going. Apostle Paul said that love is the greatest gift. "And now abide faith, hope, love, these three; but the greatest of these is love" (1 Corinthians 13:13). We need to make a commitment to love God with all our heart and soul.

God commanded us to love each other. "A new commandment I give to you, that you love one another; as I have loved you, that you also love one another. By this all will know that you are My disciples, if you have love for one another" (John 13:34–35). Examine Jesus Christ's disciples by the fruits of the Spirit—love, joy, peace, longsuffering, kindness, goodness, faithfulness, gentleness, and self-control (Galatians 5:22–23). Love, the most important spiritual fruit, edifies; all the other fruit derives from love.

First, we ought to love with words. Apostle Paul commanded that we should desire to speak edification, exhortation, and comfort to men (1 Corinthians 14:3). "Let no corrupt word proceed out of your mouth, but what is good for necessary edification, that it may impart grace to the hearers" (Ephesians 4:29). Proverbs 18:21 describes the power of tongue. "Death and life are in the power of the tongue, and those who love it will eat its fruit."

You will meet some religious people who have only enough religion to quote Bible verses but not enough religion to love. Wiersbe remarked, "Learning God's truth and getting it into our heads is one thing, but living God's truth and getting it into our characters is quite something else."[17] Don't be surprised if they teach Sunday schools, and then gossip and slander behind your back. "If anyone among you thinks he is religious, and does not bridle his tongue but deceives his own heart, this one's religion is useless" (James 1:26). If you want to know Jesus Christ's opinion of them, read Matthew 23. What will Jesus Christ do with the corrupt words they have spoken? "But I say to you that for every idle word men may speak, they will give account of it in the day of judgment" (Matthew 12:36). On a fig tree, the fruit appears at the same time as the leaves, and Jesus Christ didn't put up with a phony fig tree that only had leaves but no fruit.

> Now in the morning, as He returned to the city, He was hungry. And seeing a fig tree by the road, He came to it and found nothing on it but leaves, and said to it, "Let no fruit grow on you ever again." Immediately the fig tree withered away.
>
> Matthew 21:18–19

It is by the fruit of the Spirit that we are known as God's disciples. I am glad that those religious people still go to church; you can't find a better place for those hypocrites to go on Sunday mornings. They build up their ego by tearing down others. And yes, they too have a lot of followers; birds of a feather flock together. You will find them gathered together, talking critically about people at church and wondering why God would not use them. I pray for them a Damascus Road experience. As for me, I imitate what David did in Psalm 109:28: "Let them curse, but You bless; when they arise, let them be ashamed, but let Your servant rejoice." David asked the Lord to send him a blessing every time his enemy cursed him, as well as to bring shame to the enemy and bring him joy. I have been abundantly blessed.

Meyer commented in *Reduce Me to Love*, "One of the most amazing things I learned, one that still thrills my soul, is that Love is actually spiritual warfare."[18] All spiritual warfare starts with the mind; we also need to love with thoughts. "For to be carnally minded is death, but to be spiritually minded is life and peace" (Romans 8:6). We need to guard our mind against the devil's attacks, refuse to think the wrong thoughts when they appear, and replace them with the right ones.

> Finally, brethren, whatever things are true, whatever things are noble, whatever things are just, whatever things are pure, whatever things are lovely, whatever things are of good report, if there is any virtue and if there is anything praiseworthy—meditate on these things.
>
> Philippians 4:8

When we load our mind with God's Word and glory, we have the mind of Christ.

Thoughts, like words, affect other people. One day God told me to visit a friend, and when I went to her house, I found her in a bad mood. Even though she didn't say anything negative, by her voice tone and body language I sensed that she didn't have good thoughts of me. I seldom enjoyed our fellowship due to her critical attitude toward me and people, but I had given up people's approval and understood that I was there due to my obedience to God. I was relieved when I left her house. She didn't love me; rather, she tolerated me. I said to God, "I know your approval is all I need, but I feel very little when I am with her, knowing that she doesn't care for me."

God said, "You failed to see her faithfulness."

I need to find the good in people and let God get the bad out of them. I made a decision to think positive thoughts of her and love her. Love is a decision.

We also need to love with deeds. To love God is to obey Him and cultivate an intimate relationship with Him. Immediately after I wake up in the morning, I spend time with Him, and I study God's Word daily. I obey God moment by moment with a trusting attitude; I live on promises, not explanations. I follow Stanley's Life Principle 2, "Obey God and leave all the consequences to Him."[19] I tithe to give the first fruit to help build His kingdom. I answer God's calling to attend church and sing in the choir. I bite my tongue when I really want to say something, for He is my vindicator. I tell others what God has done for me and encourage them to walk with God. I always do those things that please Him. God is my greatest joy. "I delight to do Your will, O my God, and Your law is within my heart" (Psalm 40:8). I love God by obeying Him and giving Him my life as a living sacrifice.

I love myself. I don't allow people to abuse me verbally, and I know when I need to surround myself with people who love me through divine connection. I rest my body, soul, and mind on Saturdays. I fix myself healthy food to enjoy and pursue cooking passionately; when God allows, I eat out at my favorite restaurants. During winter, I put on my coat and enjoy a mocha frappuccino. When God tells me to go shopping, I obey and enjoy everything God gives me. I put my feet up once in a while to enjoy a clean movie. When I put gas in my car at the gas station and the radio happens to sing "Amazing Grace," I let my windows down. I cry when I hurt and laugh when I am happy. When I think of God's grace, I cry in front of the congregation at church services because it is too great for me to comprehend. I can't give people what I don't have; if I don't love myself, I can't love other people.

One day God told me to visit my eighty-six-year-old neighbor, who lives by herself. I asked God what I could do for her, and God said to bring her flowers and spend time with her. She was delighted. She talked for longer than an hour, and I listened. She told me about her deceased husband as well as other members of her family and showed me pictures of different places where her family had lived in Europe. God showed me how to love this lady, who may be lonely sometimes. Love is giving a piece of me to other people.

Apostle Paul explained love to the Corinthians when he dealt with their problems:

> Love suffers long and is kind; love does not envy; love does not parade itself, is not puffed up; does not behave rudely, does not seek its own, is not provoked, thinks no evil; does not rejoice in iniquity, but rejoices in the truth; bears all things, believes all things, hopes all things, endures all things. Love never fails ...
>
> 1 Corinthians 13:4–8

I have been learning to walk in love for almost twenty years; I am still a work in progress. Tackle one or two areas until you have made great progress, and then move on to others. It is a lifelong journey to walk in love.

Love suffers long; love is patient. Love God with patience. We should spend time with Him persistently and wait patiently for Him to mature and deliver us. In His timing we will see the visions that He has given us fulfilled.

> For My thoughts are not your thoughts, nor are your ways My ways," says the Lord. "For as the heavens are higher than the earth, so are My ways higher than your ways, and My thoughts than your thoughts.
>
> Isaiah 55:8–9

We can't figure out God's thoughts and ways; however, when we hear His still, small voice, we need to get into agreement with Him immediately, without questioning His sovereignty and love. Trust and obey. When He guides us into an unknown territory, He has already checked out the Promised Land. "My Lord, have it your way in my life," I say to the Almighty daily. I love Him with my life.

It was about ten years ago that God put the vision of a website on my heart. I used to send devotional e-mails, and when God told me to stop that ministry, I knew that He was up to something else. I waited year after year, not knowing when God was going to move. I had tried twice to implement a website; however, nothing succeeded. I then realized that it was not God's timing. In summer of 2005, God told me to start writing *The Proverbs 31 Woman* by spending a few hours working on it each weekend. In the beginning of 2006, I had also subscribed to a free website and learned how to create web pages using the embedded editors. But I didn't know when I would launch http://hisamazinggrace.org. In October 2006, God took me out of a job where I had worked for thirteen years. The second week into unemployment, God said to me, "You have time to work on that website now; go online." After I had patiently waited for almost ten years, in His timing and mysterious ways, the vision was fulfilled. I have made a commitment to follow God no matter where He leads me. I want to see all of God's plans and purposes for my life fulfilled. When I take my last breath on earth, I will have no regrets. I love the Lord, and I wait patiently for Him.

Love yourself with patience. Apostle Paul knew that we didn't have control of our sinful nature; he remarked in Romans 7:15, "For what I am doing, I do not understand. For what I will to do, that I do not practice; but what I hate, that I do." Only God can change people. Stanley said that it is not our responsibility to live the Christian life. We just need to do the best we can to obey God. I am fully aware of my weaknesses, but God will mature me from glory to glory until Jesus Christ comes back to take me home.

When you are able to love God and yourself with patience, you can then love people with patience. We need to be patient when God works in other people and help them to become all that God has created them to be. Often we are more patient with strangers than the people whom we love. The people who are close to us should have priority in our lives, but we take them for granted. Sometimes I miss my deceased parents and regret the inappropriate words I said to them when they were living. God comforts me with, "You were a typical child." Now when my son says something to hurt my feelings, I remember how I was at his age and believe that he loves me dearly.

A patient person does not complain because he is content with what he has under the circumstances; he believes that God is in control and that He has a plan. Patience is spiritual maturity. When we encounter trials, our patience is tested. When God took the Israelites out of Egypt, people complained no matter how many miracles God conducted. Wiersbe commented in *Be Exultant*, "God judged His people at Kadesh Barnea and consigned them to thirty-eight years in the wilderness while the older generation died off. It was the world's longest funeral march."[20] It took forty years for Israelites to finish an eleven days' trip due to their impatience and unbelief.

> My brethren, count it all joy when you fall into various trials, knowing that the testing of your faith produces patience. But let patience have its perfect work, that you may be perfect and complete, lacking nothing.
>
> James 1:2–4

Love is kind. "And be kind to one another, tenderhearted, forgiving one another, even as God in Christ forgave you" (Ephesians 4:32). In September of 1977, I came to United States to study for a Master of Science degree. My first impression of this country was that on Auburn University campus, people smiled and said hello, and I concluded that was how American people greeted each other. What has happened to this society? Now people put me down or talk about me instead of talking to me to get attention. One day I walked through a church parking lot toward my car, and a teenage girl looked at me and told her mom loudly that I didn't look pretty. I ignored her comments and continued to walk toward my car; she complained that I didn't talk to her after her comments. I usually don't respond to this type of manipulative behavior; if bad behavior is rewarded, how do people learn to behave better? I use this story as an example because I don't want to repeat the other cruel words I have heard. Being cruel is not cool. The Proverbs 31 woman opened her mouth with wisdom, and her speech was kind (Proverbs 31:26).

When you go to church, look for people who are new or alone and make conversation with them. Find something you like about them and give them a sincere compliment; this is a good way to start a conversation. It is also kind to help someone who looks lost. Talk to elderly people when you sense that they are lonely. When I walk around my subdivision, I make an effort to stop and talk to an elderly lady who lives alone. I make sure she understands that if she needs something, she is welcome to call me. Do not repeat rumors you have heard about other people's personal matters; better yet, refuse to listen to rumors or gossip. It is cruel to repeat rumors to destroy an innocent person's reputation.

God commands us to be kind to our enemies.

> But love your enemies, do good, and lend, hoping for nothing in return; and your reward will be

great, and you will be sons of the Most High. For
He is kind to the unthankful and evil.

Luke 6:35

Being kind to my enemies used to be difficult for me because of my expectation of people, but I am getting better at it. I did something nice for some of them, and I was relieved from bitterness and resentment. Whatever the Bible commands me to do is for my own good. To apply God's Word in my daily life, it needs to get into my heart. I will need to pray without ceasing and depend on God to change me; when God is ready to change me, I need to cooperate. If I don't make an effort, God's Word will not automatically become part of my character. When Jesus Christ was nailed on the cross, He demonstrated the greatest kindness; He said, "Father, forgive them, for they do not know what they do" (Luke 23:34).

Love does not envy. The Tenth Commandment instructs us not to covet anything that belongs to another person (Exodus 20:17). God decides what kind of gifts and talents He gives to each person; when I envy or become jealous, I fight God's will. I need to look at what God has given me and be grateful. God will never help me to become someone else, and He is big enough to love all people. God gives me the same twenty-four hours He gives Reverend Billy Graham, so I should use my time wisely to become the best me. God has already created a Graham; He needs me to be me.

Often Christians envy other people's calling; however, they don't realize what it takes for those people to work on their ministries. When my friends are out partying, I stay home to study God's Word, read everything God has told me to read, and write until I can't open my eyes. Writing in English is very hard for me because it is not my first language. However, when Jesus Christ said, "Come," I got out of the boat. Meyer said that it would cost us something to walk with God, and the price she had to pay to get into her ministry was everything she had, starting with her reputation.

Apostle Paul said:

> There are diversities of gifts, but the same Spirit. There are differences of ministries, but the same Lord. And there are diversities of activities, but it is the same God who works all in all.
>
> 1 Corinthians 12:4–6

Why do we envy? Why do we compete? Everything is from the same God and the same Spirit. Be you; don't waste your time trying to be someone else. Do your part in the body of Christ, and do the best you can to bring glory to God.

Love does not parade itself; it is not puffed up. Love God with a humble spirit and give Him the glory. It is God who equips us to do His work. We are not to be proud of what we can do; it is God who does it through us. We should use our talents and gifts to build God's kingdom and to serve people. Apostle Paul warned the proud Corinthians, "For who makes you differ from another? And what do you have that you did not receive? Now if you did indeed receive it, why do you boast as if you had not received it?" (1 Corinthians 4:7). Even though God works through people to get His job done, without God we can do nothing. Noah built the ark according to God's specifications, but on the boarding day, God caused all the animals, two by two, to come to the ark. Was it possible for Noah to do this God-size job without God? If it wasn't for God's specifications, would the ark have been safe in the flood?

"Therefore humble yourselves under the mighty hand of God, that He may exalt you in due time"(1 Peter 5:6). God won't use the proud; He can only use the humble who would give Him the glory. Pride is a difficult problem for people to deal with because it is in all of us. The greatest demonstration of humility was when Jesus Christ died on the cross. With our sinful nature, we need to rely on the Holy Spirit to keep us humble. I check my attitude daily and adjust to remain humble.

The Proverbs 31 woman humbly served her family so that her husband had time to sit among the elders of the land (Proverbs 31:23). She didn't take his place in the gates or draw attention to herself. When we serve the Lord, we are to give Him the glory, not glorify ourselves.

Love does not behave rudely. People are rude nowadays. Once in a while, when I meet people who are polite, I really enjoy them. The one thing I dislike most is gossip. Instead of talking to a person, some people talk about that person rudely to get attention. I once met a lady who would never talk to me directly about anything. While she sat next to me, she either talked to other people about her opinion of me or talked to herself and let me hear what she was saying regarding my imperfection. Gossip, nagging, and complaint are not good manners. To influence people, you need to communicate clearly and directly.

God is a spirit, and He doesn't have color. He is not white, black, or yellow. It is rude to talk about people's skin color when they can hear you. It is also rude to talk about other people's cultural background and to make them feel they aren't part of this melting pot. When church service start at nine a.m., don't show up at nine thirty a.m. It is rude to call people too early in the morning or too late at night unless it is an emergency, or to call them every day to talk about your problems. I have a tendency to interrupt people when they are talking; I am making an effort to correct myself from being rude.

Love does not seek its own; love is not selfish. If you watch how people behave, you will see selfishness. People push in front of others to get the best seat; however, love puts others first. Love also helps others grow. John Maxwell commented in *YOUR ROAD MAP FOR SUCCESS*, "The key is to find your purpose and help others while you're pursuing it."[21]

Sometimes, when God puts a vision on my heart, He will ask me to help others who are now achieving that vision in their lives. I have been singing in the church choir for more than ten years, and the desire of my heart is to sing in a Praise Team. I auditioned three times and failed at a church. I took voice lessons for a year and auditioned again, but I still failed. After God took me to a new church, I had a chance to audition for a new Praise Team; however, I got sick and had to cancel it. But I still have the burning desire to sing in a small group. Before God brings that vision to pass in my own life, He has been asking me to encourage and help others when they audition for solos. My attitude has been tested; God won't use a selfish person. He won't bring my vision to pass until I have helped enough people to achieve theirs.

Apostle Paul demonstrated great love toward the Corinthians. He didn't think of his own feelings but the feelings of others. Paul disciplined the sinned church member for his good, and after he had repented, Paul urged the church to forgive and comfort him, and to reaffirm love to him (2 Corinthians 2).

Love is not provoked; it thinks no evil. Love is not easily offended and doesn't hold a grudge. It is very hard to make friends with insecure people because they are easily offended and needy. The people who complain that I don't talk to them are the people who don't talk to me. I love all people, but I can't be all things to all people. It is not fruitful for me to be friends with some people; I can only make friends through divine connection. I do the best I can to pay attention to people no matter where I go, and I make an effort not to give offense.

People are desperate for love, and that's why they are easily offended. I do enjoy talking to people but only for a short period of time; after thirty minutes, I can feel my energy level drops. I always feel lonely among a group of people. Solitude is vital to me; however, after being alone for a while, I need to be around people. I enjoy when I spend time with just a couple of close friends. I treasure my calling to sing in the choir, but I usually feel lost among 200 people. One Wednesday evening during choir rehearsal, I was very tired from a hectic day at work and felt extremely disconnected. God told me that if I would look within for Him, I could find His presence. My distress was instantly relieved. The only person who can fill the void in each person's life is the Holy Spirit.

Do not take offense to grieve the Holy Spirit. I believe people are doing the best they can, and they can't be perfect. When people wrong me, I understand that persecution is not something strange in a devoted Christian's life and leave it to God to deal with them. This doesn't mean I don't get hurt once in a while; it only means that when I am hurt, I immediately go to God in prayer and seek His comfort. The Lord is my shepherd; He restores my soul.

Love does not rejoice in iniquity but rejoices in the truth. If we love the Lord, we must hate evil. Most people know that they shouldn't murder, but they don't know what their tongue can do. In this society, slander is acceptable even at church. I often hear people slander someone else and say, "She is my friend." I think, *If she has a friend like you, she does not need enemies.* Do not glorify yourself at the expense of your friends. I usually stand up for the people who are under attack by their *friends*; I have no respect for unfaithful people. Some people even told me that slander is part of the culture. I don't think it is a cultural problem; rather, it is an integrity issue. Jesus Christ's disciples ought to have integrity when they deal with people.

> And the tongue is a fire, a world of iniquity.
> The tongue is so set among our members that
> it defiles the whole body, and sets on fire the
> course of nature; and it is set on fire by hell.
>
> James 3:6

There was sexual immorality in the Corinthians' church; a man had his father's wife (1 Corinthians 5:1). Wiersbe remarked that instead of mourning, the people at Corinth were puffed up. They were boasting of the fact that their church was so "open-minded" that even fornicators could be members in good standing. You can see injustice and immorality everywhere; Christians, stand up for what is right. When you keep silent, you agree with what has been done or said. Let's encourage each other to be the change this society needs. You are the light in this dark world.

God hates sin but loves the sinners. God sent Abraham to Canaan, and there was a famine. Instead of staying, he went down to Egypt where he suffered from Pharaoh and his officers. But God intervened and took him out of the situation that would have changed God's plan; if Sarah had become one of Pharaoh's wives, that would have changed the plan of the promised Messiah. Abraham repented and went back to Canaan. God didn't like Abraham's sin, but He loved Abraham. Everything Abraham received in Egypt later caused problems; disobedience led to heartache. Pharaoh gave Abraham a lot of wealth and Sarah an Egyptian maid, Hagar. Because of the wealth, Abraham and Lot had to separate, and Hagar gave birth to Ishmael. God forgave Abraham, and he pleased God by seeking peace with Lot when there was strife between their herdsmen. Abraham let Lot choose the plain of Jordan; it was well watered everywhere. He let God choose for himself. God gave Abraham all the land he could see and countless descendants. God's promises to Abraham came to pass as he obeyed God in faith: "I will make you a great nation; I will bless you and make your name great; and you shall be a blessing" (Genesis 12:2). Jesus Christ was the only perfect lamb; all of us have sinned against God. Once we repent from our wicked ways, God can use us in a great way.

Love bears all things, believes all things, hopes all things, and endures all things. We need to believe the sovereignty and perfect love of God so that we can bear and endure the trials of life. Wiersbe commented,

> Tests often follow triumphs. This principle is illustrated in the history of Israel. No sooner had the nation been delivered from Egypt than the Egyptian army chased them and cornered them at the Red Sea (Ex.12–15). Triumph was followed by testing. God brought them through, but then they faced another test: no water (15:22–27). After that came hunger (Ex.16) and an attack from the Amalekites (Ex.17). Tests follow triumphs.[22]

We grow in faith by going through trial, another trial, and more trials. Stanley remarked in *THE BLESSINGS OF BROKENNESS,*

> One of the things I have discovered through being broken, however, is that after brokenness we can experience God's greatest blessings. After brokenness our lives can be the most fruitful and have the most purpose. The dawn after a very dark and storm-wreaked night is glorious.[23]

He also commented, "Our role in times of brokenness is to submit not only to what God desires to do in our lives, but also to his timetable."[24]

I am not telling you that I enjoy being broken by God; when I see brokenness coming again, I dread. But I have learned to make the best out of the situation and get excited with anticipation that God will work all things for my good and His glory. It takes courage and patience to endure brokenness; this is when the root of faith grows deeper. I have learned to look at the big picture of God's will instead of the closed door and the uncomfortable circumstances, and I rejoice in the blessings each day brings. When I first believed in God, He nourished me with blessings and miracles. After a while, He began to ask me to make some sacrifices, like taking the China mission trip, giving away my favorite possessions, and taking care of people I didn't particularly like. The severe trials came after I started to send devotional e-mails. I knew that the devil attacked me for what I was doing for God; every day I struggled through the strange things that happened to me. I went to department stores, and people there recognized me and cursed me. I was thinking about an issue in my mind at work, and the co-worker who sat in the next cube said aloud what was in my mind. Some incidents happened in the church choir, and I heard people talking about it at the Starbucks drive-thru window twenty miles away. The devil is real. For many years I went through one trial after another, and some mornings I didn't know if I was able to get up. But when I saw what God was doing with the e-mails I sent, my heart burned with fire to tell people about my Lord. Through the triumph of each trial, my faith in God grows deeper, and I grow spiritually. I have experienced the blessings of brokenness, and I am now excited to see what God is doing in my life through each challenge. I believe in God's love in the midst of painful trials; all things work for good.

Love believes the best in everyone. Most of the time, people aren't out there to hurt you. Hurting people hurt people; they have so much pain inside that they have to let the pain out somehow. For the people who had been used by the devil to hurt me, I have prayed the same prayer Jesus Christ did on the cross. "Father, forgive them, for they do not know what they do." If their intention was to hurt me, God is my vindicator. I am free to love people without worrying about getting hurt. I am not saying you ought to be a doormat. Use your discernment in abusive situations.

Love is unnatural for our sinful nature; we can only love through the strength of the Holy Spirit, who lives in us. Only when we receive the love of God can His love then flow out of us to others. God is love, and when we love others, God is with us. "And walk in love, as Christ also has loved us and given Himself for us, an offering and a sacrifice to God for a sweet-smelling aroma" (Ephesians 5:2).

Love was the pure motive of the Proverbs 31 woman. She loved the Lord, and that's why she obeyed Him to be a submissive wife and loving mother without glorifying herself. Love motivated her to work. This unselfish love made her the role model of Christian women.

Live a Joyful Life

It is God's will that we live a joyful life. " … I have come that they may have life, and that they may have it more abundantly" (John 10:10). When we have a personal relationship with God, life is to be enjoyed as a gift from Him; however, if we don't fear God and obey His commandments, life is vanity.

> If you keep My commandments, you will abide in My love, just as I have kept My Father's commandments and abide in His love. These things I have spoken to you, that My joy may remain in you, and that your joy may be full.
>
> John 15:10–11

I started to question my identity during the first few years at elementary school in Taiwan. I wondered why I existed and was born as me, not as someone else. In high school I encountered Rene Descartes' "I think, therefore I am"; however, I ended up with more unanswered questions. If I don't think, do I not exist? Rene only claimed the existence of himself, and he wasn't saying that his existence was necessary. Is life worth living? For centuries, philosophers tried to uncover the meaning of human existence. King Solomon had everything, and yet he said his life was empty. After my Savior came into my life, I realized that I was created by the Creator of the Universe for a specific purpose.

> For You formed my inward parts; You covered me in my mother's womb. I will praise You, for

> I am fearfully and wonderfully made; marvelous are Your works, and that my soul knows very well. My frame was not hidden from You, when I was made in secret, and skillfully wrought in the lowest parts of the earth.
>
> Psalm 139:13–15

Wiersbe commented, "No Christian should ever complain to God because of his lack of gifts or abilities, or because of his limitations or handicaps. Psalm 139:13–16 indicates that our very genetic structure is in the hands of God. Each of us must accept himself and be himself."[25] The only way to live a joyful life is to accept God's creation that we all have a unique purpose in the body of Christ and know that life is meaningless and short unless we live to glorify the Lord. My favorite uncle passed away recently, and I grieved that I lost another loved one after my parents. However, God is in control of birth and death. "A time to be born, and a time to die" (Ecclesiastes 3:2). Live for God and enjoy daily adventure, for He gives us richly all things to enjoy (1 Timothy 6:17).

God made me a Computer System Engineer. I don't know everything about computers, but God equips me for the assignments He calls me to do. I sometimes wish I was a Broadway singer or pilot; however, when God designed me in my mother's womb, He had a different idea. Singing is my hobby, but I am not good enough to sing in the Broadway shows. I am content to sing in the church choir to worship God. I don't think I will ever become a pilot; it is not part of my genetic makeup. When I worked at Lockheed Martin

Aeronautical Systems, I e-mailed an *F*-22 test pilot to see if he would give me a ride when he flew his *F*-22. He wasn't agreeable, not even after I offered to give him a dollar for the ride. But he signed an *F*-22 poster for me, and I was delighted. I am not athletic. If you ask me if I play tennis, I will answer, "Tennis plays me!" I don't drive very well and am not very good with directions; you can see why I am not interested in racing cars. As I mature emotionally and spiritually, I accept and am grateful for my God given gifts and talents and my unique purpose in the body of Christ. Because I am fearfully and wonderfully made by God, I have learned to appreciate the person He created in me. Whatever I can't do, God has created others to do it. "Let us not become conceited, provoking one another, envying one another" (Galatians 5:26). I wait with great anticipation for God to unfold the rest of my life as I continue to be myself and be all that I can be.

It is God's will that we enjoy work and life.

> So I commended enjoyment, because a man has nothing better under the sun than to eat, drink, and be merry; for this will remain with him in his labor all the days of his life which God gives him under the sun.
>
> Ecclesiastes 8:15

When we see our work as a gift of God through most of our days on earth, we can enjoy God's abundant provision of life. After God created man, male and female—

> Then God blessed them, and God said to them, "Be fruitful and multiply; fill the earth and subdue it; have dominion over the fish of the sea, over the birds of the air, and over every living thing that moves on the earth."
>
> Genesis 1:28

The first thing God said to Adam and Eve was "Go to work." The Proverbs 31 woman was a beautiful, energetic, and strong worker. She demonstrated love for labor. She worked to provide clothing and food for her family and watched over her home; she was also an industrious woman who had her own business (Proverbs 31:13–27). We should see the job that God has assigned to us a privilege to serve and work heartily for Him. We should also enjoy the fruits of our labor and live a balanced, joyful life.

Our lives should be fruitful but not too busy. Abide in God and find rest in obedience. When I joined FBA, I prayed for God to show me if He wanted me to be in the choir; I had been in the choir for more than ten years at the other church. Choir is a huge commitment. God revealed His will to me, and I joined the choir joyfully. It is the desire of my heart to serve Him with singing. Sometimes people invite me to other church activities, which is a good thing; however, if it is not God's will, then it is not my calling. I have to say no to the good things and only say yes to God. I rest my spirit in God's will and trust Him to direct, provide, and protect; the Lord is my shepherd (Psalm 23:1).

There is joy in serving God if we do things God's way and rely on the power of the Holy Spirit. We can't depend on our flesh or other resources to accomplish God's work. "...'Not by might nor by power, but by My Spirit,' says the Lord of hosts" (Zechariah 4:6). Wiersbe quoted,

> "We say we depend on the Holy Spirit," wrote Vance Havner, "but actually we are so wired up with our own devices that if the fire does not fall from heaven, we can turn on a switch and produce false fire of our own. If there is no sound of a rushing mighty wind, we have the furnace all set to blow hot air instead. God save us from a synthetic Pentecost!"[26]

When we obey, God is with us and rejoices over us; by the power of the Holy Spirit, we will succeed. "The Lord your God in your midst, The Mighty One, will save; He will rejoice over you with gladness, He will quiet you with His love, He will rejoice over you with singing" (Zephaniah 3:17).

"This is the day the Lord has made; we will rejoice and be glad in it" (Psalm 118:24). Live one day at a time. God only gives us grace for today. Yesterday ended last night, and tomorrow will come if God is willing. "Therefore do not worry about tomorrow, for tomorrow will worry about its own things. Sufficient for the day is its own trouble" (Matthew 6:34). Focusing only on today will take a lot of stress off our lives. Abide in God, and He will guide your path for today. This doesn't mean we don't plan for the future; we should focus and enjoy the things at hand.

Most of our days are ordinary. We shouldn't despise the ordinary chaos in life. Do ordinary things in an extraordinary way. Be creative and have fun. Find a different way to drive to work, learn a new dish once a month, make a new friend, go extra miles for an old friend, learn a new skill, try a new hairstyle, do something that you don't usually do, and change your perspective on something that bothers you. No one is responsible for your joy but you. Don't let other people steal your joy; set healthy boundaries. Joy has nothing to do with the circumstances; it is what happens inside of you. Don't wait for joy to come one day; live today to its fullest.

Rest is essential to live a joyful life.

> Come to Me, all you who labor and are heavy laden, and I will give you rest. Take My yoke upon you and learn from Me, for I am gentle and lowly in heart, and you will find rest for your souls.
>
> Matthew 11:28–29

We should be led by God to rest our body and soul. I rest my physical body periodically during the day and keep a regular bed time. I sleep well because I know that God stays awake and watches over me, and when I wake up, He is there to greet me. "He will not allow your foot to be moved; He who keeps you will not slumber. Behold, He who keeps Israel shall neither slumber nor sleep" (Psalm 121:3–4). I also rest on the Sabbath day, which is Saturday for me. When I don't feel good physically, I can't have joy. God also protects my emotions; He restores my soul (Psalm 23:3).

The storms of life will come, and we need to rest in God. "Peace I leave with you, My peace I give to you; not as the world gives do I give to you. Let not your heart be troubled, neither let it be afraid" (John 14:27). Trials and persecution are not strange things in a Christian's life; expect them. God allows trials to come to me to test my faith, bring me closer to Him, and prepare me for future services. Stanley said that we ought to be thankful that God trusts us with the trials; he remarked, "The joy set before us, however, is the joy of knowing that God is with us, working in us and through us, and that God is pleased with us." Relax and sit at the right hand of God with Jesus Christ. During the storms, always remember: "And we know that all things work together for good to those who love God, to those who are the called according to His purpose" (Romans 8:28).

"If you abide in Me, and My words abide in you, you will ask what you desire, and it shall be done for you" (John 15:7). Do not strive; abide in God. When we stay in close fellowship with God and are committed to doing things God's way, His desire will become ours, and all things shall be done in His ways and timing. There is a promise to the believers: "Until now you have asked nothing in My name. Ask, and you will receive, that your joy may be full" (John 16:24). God will provide all we need. All we have to do is ask in His will and believe that we will receive.

The cost of our salvation was God's only son, and it was because of God's mercy and grace that we received from Him. "Assuredly, I say to you, whoever does not receive the kingdom of God as a little child will by no means enter it" (Luke 18:17). This doesn't mean we don't have to do our part; we need to do our part only and let

God be God. He will do His part. When we abide in God, we are relaxed and do only what God tells us to do. We then receive what God wants us to have joyfully. Anything beyond God's will requires a lot of effort to maintain, and it is not our best.

We shall only expect God to meet our needs rather than people. "My soul, wait silently for God alone, for my expectation is from him" (Psalm 62:5). God uses people to meet our needs; however, we must understand that it is God who provides through people. Most of the time, God uses the most impossible people. He has multiple purposes in whatever He does. Receive His best choices with confidence that He has our best in mind, even though they may not be our choices. Receive His love joyfully, and focus on His will for your life.

It is a joy to receive, but it is a greater joy to be a blessing. God blesses us that we might be a blessing to others. Walk in love and help others to become all that they can be. I obey God to make friends with individuals that I may be a blessing to them. I obey God's instruction to give money and material things to others. I have been a Joyce Meyer Ministry partner for a long time, and I share her teaching resources with others to help them grow spiritually. Joyce Meyer Ministries took a group of medical staff to Africa to fulfill the unmet needs in those people's life, and I am blessed that I had the privilege to contribute to that effort. I am also a long-time In Touch Ministry donor, and I am blessed when I see how the Ministry grows and brings people worldwide closer to God. I am sharing what God has taught me in this book, that I may bless others with my personal testimonies. It is a great joy to serve God and fellow Christians and to bring the unsaved into God's kingdom.

When we have acquaintances and friends to share our life and blessings with, the joy is multiplied. Make an effort to develop relationships with people around you. A mature Christian gets along with others if possible. As long as we are in a relationship, we will get hurt. Our capacity to build relationships depends on our capacity to forgive. As for the people who hurt us intentionally, God is our vindicator. "Wait on the Lord, and keep His way, and He shall exalt you to inherit the land; when the wicked are cut off, you shall see it" (Psalm 37:34).

To live a joyful life, we will have to mind our own business. Some people spend most of their time interfering with other people's affairs; they don't do what they are supposed to do. If we don't mind our own business, it is possible for any religious activity to become a gossip center. The people who are busy doing God's work don't have time to gossip or mingle in other people's business. Look at the Proverbs 31 woman; she didn't even have time to be idle (Proverbs 31:27).

> That you also aspire to lead a quiet life, to mind your own business, and to work with your own hands, as we commanded you, that you may walk properly toward those who are outside, and that you may lack nothing.
>
> 1 Thessalonians 4:11

The most joyful thing for a Christian is to worship, praise God, and give thanks to God for all things at all times.

> Speaking to one another in psalms and hymns
> and spiritual songs, singing and making melody in
> your heart to the Lord, giving thanks always for all
> things to God the Father in the name of our Lord
> Jesus Christ.
>
> Ephesians 5:19–20

God puts songs in our hearts, and we sing them to give thanks. We shall finish our earthly journey with joy. "For you shall go out with joy, and be led out with peace; the mountains and the hills shall break forth into singing before you, and all the trees of the field shall clap their hands" (Isaiah 55:12).

What joy to be in a personal relationship with the Lord! We will receive our harvest. "Give her of the fruit of her hands, and let her own works praise her in the gates" (Proverbs 31:31). God calls all the Christian women to praise the Proverbs 31 woman and to become her. Her children called her blessed, and her husband praised her (Proverbs 31: 28). The other people in the community praised her (Proverbs 31:31). But the most important voice of praise came from God, "Charm is deceitful and beauty is passing, but a woman who fears the Lord, she shall be praised" (Proverbs 31:30).

From the desk of Tiffany Chen

Dear Friend,

If you have not invited Jesus Christ to be your Lord and Savior, I encourage you to do so now. I know that your life is difficult because I used to be there. I used to live with fear and uncertainty, not knowing what the future would hold. Jesus Christ touched my heart one day, and I entered a personal relationship with Him. My life was changed forever. You may be skeptical like I used to be, but the truth is that you have nothing to lose. Why don't you give yourself a chance to receive salvation? All you have to do is receive Jesus Christ into your heart.

Father, I pray for you to touch my reader right now the same way you touched me twenty years ago. Bring him/her into a close relationship with you, and love and bless him/her abundantly.

My friend, bow your head now and receive Jesus Christ as your Lord. Find a church home that teaches God's Word, and start a new life. You will never regret it if you give yourself a chance for a blessed life.

In His Love,

Tiffany

End Notes

1 Warren Wiersbe, *The Warren Wiersbe BE Collection W/ QuickVerse* 2005, http://www.quickverse.com

2 Warren W. Wiersbe, *Be Worshipful* (Colorado Springs: Victor, 2004), 26

3 Warren W. Wiersbe, *The Bible Exposition Commentary Volume* 2 (Wheaton: Victor Books, 1989), 516

4 John C. Maxwell, *TODAY MATTERS* (New York: Center Street, 2004), 228

5 John C. Maxwell, *TODAT MATTERS* (New York: Center Street, 2004), 228

6 Tim LaHAYE, *Spirit-Controlled Temperament* (Wheaton: Tyndale House Publishers, Inc. 1992), 1–7

7 Tim LaHAYE, *Spirit-Controlled Temperament* (Wheaton: Tyndale House Publishers, Inc. 1992), 11–39

8 Warren W. Wiersbe, *The Bible Exposition Commentary Volume* 1 (Wheaton: Victor Books, 1989), 466

9   Charles Stanley, *Life Principles Bible* (Nashville: Thomas Nelson, Inc, 2005), xxxv

10 Warren W. Wiersbe, *The Bible Exposition Commentary Volume* 1 (Wheaton: Victor Books, 1989), 469

11 Warren W. Wiersbe, *The Bible Exposition Commentary Volume* 1 (Wheaton: Victor Books, 1989), 355

12 Warren W. Wiersbe, *The Bible Exposition Commentary Volume* 1 (Wheaton: Victor Books, 1989), 355

13 Warren W. Wiersbe, *The Bible Exposition Commentary Volume* 1 (Wheaton: Victor Books, 1989), 572

14 John Revere, *THE BAIT OF SATAN* (Lake Mary: Charisma House, 2004), 252

15 Warren Wiersbe, *The Warren Wiersbe BE Collection W/ QuickVerse* 2005, http://www.quickverse.com

16 Warren W. Wiersbe, *Be Worshipful* (Colorado Springs: Victor, 2004), 201

17 Warren W. Wiersbe, *The Bible Exposition Commentary Volume* 1 (Wheaton: Victor Books, 1989), 631

18 Joyce Meyer, *Reduce Me to Love* (New York: Time Warren Book Group, 2000), 141

19 Charles Stanley, *Life Principles Bible* (Nashville: Thomas Nelson, Inc, 2005), xviii

20 Warren W. Wiersbe, *Be Exultant* (Colorado Springs: Victor, 2004), 29

21 John Maxwell, *YOUR ROAD MAP FOR SUCCESS* (Nashville: Thomas Nelson, Inc. 2002), 17

22 Warren Wiersbe, *The Warren Wiersbe BE Collection W/ QuickVerse* 2005, http://www.quickverse.com

23 Charles Stanley, *THE BLESSINGS OF BROKENNESS* (Grand Rapids: Zondervan, 1997), 10

24 Charles Stanley, *THE BLESSINGS OF BROKENNESS* (Grand Rapids: Zondervan, 1997), 60

25 Warren W. Wiersbe, *The Bible Exposition Commentary Volume* 1 (Wheaton: Victor Books, 1989), 642

26 Warren Wiersbe, *The Warren Wiersbe BE Collection W/ QuickVerse* 2005, http://www.quickverse.com

Scripture Index

Bibliography

LaHaye, Tim. *Spirit-Controlled Temperament.* Wheaton: Tyndale House Publishers, Inc. 1992.

LaHaye, Tim. *How to Study the Bible for Yourself.* Eugene: Harvest House Publishers, 1998.

Lewis, Eleanor. *How to Accept Yourself, Understand Others, and Like Them Anyway!!!.* Marietta: Insights &Beginnings, 1998.

Maxwell, John. *Your Road Map For Success.* Nashville: Thomas Nelson, Inc. 2002.

Maxwell, John C. *Today Matters.* New York: Center Street, 2004.

Meyer, Joyce. *Reduce Me to Love.* New York: Time Warren Book Group, 2000.

Revere, John. *The Bait Of Satan.* Lake Mary: Charisma House, 2004.

Stanley, Charles. *The Blessings Of Brokenness.* Grand Rapids: Zondervan, 1997.

Stanley, Charles. *Life Principles Bible.* Nashville: Thomas Nelson, Inc, 2005.

Wiersbe, Warren W. *The Bible Exposition Commentary Volume* 1. Wheaton: Victor Books, 1989.

Wiersbe, Warren W. *The Bible Exposition Commentary Volume* 2. Wheaton: Victor Books, 1989.

Wiersbe, Warren W. *Be Exultant.* Colorado Springs: Victor, 2004.

Wiersbe, Warren W. *Be Worshipful.* Colorado Springs: Victor, 2004.

Wiersbe, Warren. *The Warren Wiersbe BE Collection W/ QuickVerse* 2005, http://www.quickverse.com